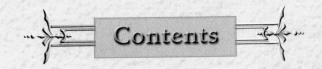

Contents

Dedication

To Lila and Mark Rosenweig,
who have always showed interest
and support in our writing,
and Roxanne,
the newest member of our family.

About the Authors

Susan and Jim Harran, antique dealers of "A Moment In Time," specialize in English and continental porcelains and antique cups and saucers. The Harrans have authored four books, entitled *Collectible Cups and Saucers Books I, II,* and *III,* and *Dresden Porcelain Studios.* They write feature articles for various antique publications and have a monthly column in *AntiqueWeek,* entitled "The World of Ceramics." Susan is a member of the Antique Appraisal Association of America Inc., and they are both members of the Antiques & Collectibles Dealer Association. The Harrans display their antiques at some of the top antique shows in the country. They also do business on the Internet. Their website is www.tias.com/stores/amit. The Harrans enjoy traveling around the country to keep abreast of trends in the antiques marketplace. They reside in Neptune, New Jersey.

Acknowledgments

First and foremost, we'd like to thank the members of the staff of Collector Books. If it had not been for our publisher Bill Schroeder, our editor Gail Ashburn, and her assistant Amy Sullivan, this book would not have been possible. We appreciate the beautiful cover design by Beth Summers and the book design by Marty Turner. The staff at Collector Books is professional, talented, and always helpful.

We would like to express our appreciation to those collectors and dealers who so generously gave of their time and knowledge to make this book a reality. We are indebted to Heinz Barfuss of Lollar, Germany. We were unable to make a trip to Germany, and Heinz was our "eyes and ears." He was kind enough to take a trip to Meissen for us with his wife Heidi and daughter Lisa. He sent us beautiful photographs of the town of Meissen, the manufactory buildings, Exhibition Hall, and various artists making and decorating porcelain in the showroom. We appreciate the professional quality of Heinz's photography.

Once again we would like to thank Nina and Joe Som of Tri State Antiques, Prospect Park, Pennsylvania, for sending us photographs of some of their exceptional Meissen figures and decorative pieces. Meissen pieces of this quality and condition are rare, and we thank the Soms for sharing them with us.

A special thank you to our good friend Richard Rendall of Cincinnati, Ohio, for sending us some photographs from his lovely collection. We always enjoy sharing information about hand-painted porcelain with Richard.

Many thanks to Mary and Terry Eletheriou of MTE Antiques, Norwalk, Connecticut. They let us come in their booth during a show to photograph some of their lovely Meissen figures. We appreciate their help.

A special thanks to our friend, Charlene Margiotta, for her professional illustrations of many of the Meissen marks in our book. Charlene is a professional artist/graphic designer and can be reached at Art & Design Studio of Rockland, 149 Middletown Road, Nanuet, New York 10954, 845-624-2426.

We would like to express our sincere appreciation to our friends at Meissen, Inc., New York, for their help and hospitality. We appreciate Peter H. Jungkunst taking the time to answer our questions, giving us research material, and allowing us the opportunity to photograph many lovely pieces in his showroom. A special thank you to the new president, Sabine Collins, and her assistant, Beverly Pfahlert, for their ongoing help.

Lastly, we again thank Todd Robertson, owner of Sure Service Photo in Neptune, New Jersey, and the members of the staff, Barbara and Marie, for their support in our challenging task. They were never too busy to process our film in a professional and timely manner.

Preface

Meissen porcelain is eagerly collected throughout the world. It is traded vigorously at antique shows, auctions, and on the Internet. As antique dealers for 23 years, we have always loved the wonderful porcelains made at Meissen because of their fine hand painting and gilt detail. No two pieces are alike because everything at Meissen is done by hand. We believe Meissen employed the best flower, portrait, and figure artists of the day. Meissen porcelain itself is unique. It is harder, whiter, and more translucent than that made by other porcelain manufacturers.

There are a number of books available on Meissen, but to our knowledge there is only one other price guide. We believed there was a need for a book featuring everyday items available in the marketplace instead of the eighteenth century museum pieces found in most Meissen books, and we decided to write one. The majority of our pieces date from the mid-nineteenth century through the 1950s. All of the over 600 photographs in the book were taken from pieces that have been in our inventory or that of other dealers and collectors. We have tried to establish a realistic market price range.

The purpose of this book is to provide, all in one source, historical information about the beautiful city of Meissen and a brief history of the Meissen manufactory itself, from the discovery of white gold by Johann Friedrich Böttger to Meissen's goals and operation today. We discuss Meissen's proud, prosperous days and its periods of low morale and economic decline. We show how Meissen has weathered wars and depressions and how today it has gained international fame for outstanding production over its long and unique history. We explain how Meissen porcelain is made, discuss European decorating styles, and give examples of Meissen's most popular shapes. We have included a helpful marks section.

We include a section on decorative porcelain and discuss some of the popular motifs, such as birds, hunting, Watteau courting scenes, landscapes, and portrait items. We include dinnerware services, massive vases and centerpieces, figural sweet meat bowls, tureens, and other decorative items.

We include several chapters on one of Meissen's most important decorative motifs — flowers. We include Deutsch Blumen and Strewn and Applied Flowers. We include the popular Rose and Vine Leaf patterns. Floral decorations made Meissen famous right from the beginning.

The demand for Oriental porcelain was great in the eighteenth century, and we show how Meissen copied many early Chinese and Japanese patterns. We include the popular Indian patterns: Indian Flowers, Dragon patterns, the Yellow Lion pattern, and Kakiemon decoration. At present Meissen carries more than 250 kinds of Indian painting.

Meissen's Blue Onion pattern, the company's most recognized pattern, has endured for over 250 years. We include its history, explain the decoration, symbolism, and changes to the pattern, and take a look at Blue Onion today. We also discuss some of the other companies who have copied the Blue Onion pattern.

The book contains a chapter on Meissen figures, highlighting the most famous figure modelers at Meissen. Famous series including Court Life, Italian Comedy, Country Life, Street Traders, Cupids, and Artisans are discussed. We personally collect the Hentschel babies and have included photographs from our collection. We cover some of Meissen's famous animal series, such as the popular monkey band, birds, and the pug dog.

Meissen porcelains have been popular since the outset of their production in the early eighteenth century, and many companies throughout Europe copied Meissen's patterns. We discuss English, French, and German copycats, especially the Dresden studios. There are still misunderstandings about Meissen and Dresden porcelains, and we try to clear up the confusion.

We were fortunate to visit the Meissen porcelain office in New York and were able to take home some helpful Meissen pattern books and source materials, as well as photograph many lovely pieces that are in Meissen's current inventory. We've provided useful information for the collector and dealer and a helpful index.

Many publications and Internet sites have supplied helpful information, and these sources are acknowledged in the bibliography. We hope this book will make it easier for the beginning as well as the advanced collector, dealer, and appraiser, to identify and price Meissen porcelains. We realize that in a book of this nature and scope, some degree of error is unavoidable, and we apologize in advance.

We would appreciate hearing your comments, and our address is below. If you would like a reply, please include a self-addressed, stamped envelope.

Jim and Susan Harran
208 Hemlock Drive
Neptune, NJ 07753

Meissen: Famous Porcelain City

The city of Meissen is located northeast of Dresden where the Triebisch River flows into the Elbe River in east central Germany. Meissen is in Saxony which is in the very heart of Europe, bordered by other German regions, the Czech Republic, and Poland. The Elbe is its main river and eastern Europe's most direct trade route to the Atlantic Ocean.

The countryside around Meissen is partly plains and partly mountainous with fertile lands, rich pastures, and vineyards. Vineyards have been in operation for hundreds of years and were first owned by monasteries. Meissen wine is well known throughout Germany.

Abundant deposits of silver, tin, iron, copper, and precious stones were discovered in Saxony during the Middle Ages. Mining became an important industry and was the major reason for Saxony's wealth.

In 929 King Henry I built a fortress on a rocky plateau in Saxony, and the town of Meissen grew up around the foot-hills of the castle. Around the year 1000 Meissen was granted a decree permitting settlement and holding its own markets. In 1150 it was first officially documented as a town.

Germany

Plate with hand-painted view of Albrechtsburg.

Famous Landmarks

Albrechtsburg

The Albrechtsburg was first built in 929, and the adjoining cathedral was added in 1260. It is the first castle to be used as a royal residence in Germany. In the late fifteenth century Duke Albert the Brave (1486 – 1500) commissioned the architect, Arnold of Westphalia, who was called the master of the vault technique, to rebuild an impressive fortress for his residence. The entire complex, including fortress, cathedral, and the bishop's castle became the symbol of the city of Meissen and was called Albrechtsburg (Albert's fortress) in 1676. The method of construction, including the draped-arch windows, was considered modern for that time. The cathedral is a wonderful example of mid-Gothic architecture. The Prince's Chapel is one of the most famous burial places of the Wettin family.

Front view of Albrechtsburg Cathedral West

View of Albrechtsburg from opposite Elbe River bank.

Albrechtsburg, 1902 German postcard.

Great banquet room in Albrechtsburg, 1902 German postcard.

Church of Our Lady (Frauenkirche)

Church of Our Lady in background.

This famous Meissen landmark is situated in the old marketplace. It has a 57 meter tower. It was founded in 1258 and is the town museum today. The church has the world's first working bells made of Meissen porcelain which were installed in a clock in the church tower in 1929. The bells crack regularly and are replaced at no charge by the Meissen factory.

Town Hall

Crossed swords emblem on town hall.

Gothic town hall.

The Gothic town hall was built in 1479 and restored in 1875. It is located in the marketplace. It has a gold crossed swords emblem on one of the dormers.

The City of Meissen Today

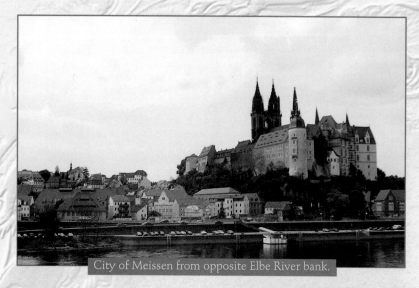

City of Meissen from opposite Elbe River bank.

Main shopping alley toward castle.

Albrechtsburg Medieval Festival, May 1, 2004.

Today the city has over 37,000 inhabitants. Many Meissen buildings reflect the Renaissance style and include townhouses with beautiful cross vaults, elaborate spiral staircases, and sculptures. The colorful town has narrow medieval streets and alleys, and the central square is surrounded by shops, cafés, and wine taverns. The Albrechtsburg Medieval Festival is held in the town square annually in May. Thousands of visitors come to Meissen each year to visit the Albrechtsburg, the churches and the most famous porcelain factory in the world — Meissen porcelain.

Carriage (droschke) for sightseeing along Meissen's cobblestone streets.

Old brick nineteenth century townhouse.

The Eighteenth Century: The Beginning

The Discovery of White Gold

An important incentive for the development of porcelain, or "white gold" as it was referred to in the eighteenth century, was the passion of King Augustus II for porcelain — a passion that almost amounted to a sickness. Augustus II, also known as Augustus the Strong, was King of Poland and the elector of Saxony in the last decade of the seventeenth century.

Augustus II is considered the most popular Saxon ruler, actively contributing to the development of Dresden as an important center of cultural, intellectual, and artistic life in Europe. He was a much more enlightened ruler than his contemporaries. He had a keen interest in science and the arts, and encouraged his leading technologists to meet and exchange ideas. He was also one of the most immoral rulers in Europe and was said to have fathered 354 illegitimate children, which earned him the title of Augustus the Strong.

Saxony was not rich, and Augustus II always needed money. In 1701 he heard of a young alchemist, Johann Friedrich Böttger (1682 – 1719), who boasted that he could produce gold from base metals. Böttger, fearing imprisonment due to his failure to make gold in Berlin, had fled to Saxony. Augustus II took him into custody and ordered him to produce gold. After Böttger's experiments also failed at the Saxon Court, Augustus II placed him under the supervision of Ehrenfried Walther von Tschirnhaus (1651 – 1708) who was a Saxon mathematician and physicist of international renown. Their task was to invent "white gold" similar to that made by the Chinese.

"J. F. Böttger has discovered the formula for making porcelain in 1709." (French trade card)

Augustus II ordered Böttger and his team to work in isolation in the medieval fortress, Albrechtsburg. As a forerunner of porcelain, the team produced a brown earthenware that was fired at a very high temperature and not permeable to water. Due to its hardness and color this material was called Jasper Porcelain by Böttger.

In 1707 Böttger was brought back to the castle in Dresden to live in a closely guarded laboratory in the Venus Tower. It was in this fume laden, unhealthy lab that Böttger, assisted by his fellow workers, achieved world fame. A white earth known as "schnorrsche weise erde" had been discovered in Seilitz, about seven and a half miles from Meissen. This clay was called kaolin, and Böttger and his colleagues fired it along with a mixture of other ingredients, including alabaster, at high temperatures. The result was the first European hard-paste porcelain.

On March 28, 1709, Böttger sent a message to Augustus II. It informed the king that he had invented a white porcelain as good as, if not superior to, the Chinese one. On January 23, 1710 it was proudly announced in four languages that the elector of Saxony and King of Poland planned to establish a porcelain manufactory that would make porcelain equaling that made in Eastern Asia.

The manufactory began operations on June 6, 1710, in Meissen in the Gothic fortress Albrechtsburg. It was selected for several reasons. First, it could be easily guarded in order to protect the secret of porcelain manufacturing. Second, the wood needed to operate the

"Augustus II traded the King of Prussia a regiment of soldiers for four dozen Chinese porcelain items." (French trade card)

ceramic kilns could easily be transported over the Elbe River. Finally, it was close to the town of Seilitz, where kaolin was mined.

The Meissen work force consisted of 23 men, all working prisoners who were not artists, but very good craftsman. This was the beginning of the greatest ceramic enterprise in Europe.

Böttger did not live long enough to see the triumph of his invention, but he realized its importance. When speaking about porcelain, it is reported that he said:

"There are three things whereby men are moved to desire this or that object which otherwise is not needful for their use: (1) beauty (2) scarcity (3) the exchange value that attached to these properties."

Böttger died at the young age of 37.

Böttger Memorial, opposite Meissen factory entrance.

The Golden Age of Meissen

"The Meissen porcelain from Böttger to Kaendler has an artistic brilliance, originality and quality which is pure genius. The products from this period are rightly termed the Golden Age."

GEOFFREY GODDEN, *GODDEN'S GUIDE TO EUROPEAN PORCELAIN*

The success of the Meissen manufactory after 1720 inflamed the King's passion for collecting porcelain. In a letter to Count Flemming on May 22, 1726 he wrote, "Are you not aware that the same is true for oranges as for porcelain; that once one has the sickness of one or the other, one can never get enough of the things and wishes to have more and more."

Two men were hired that had perhaps the greatest influence on the new Meissen manufactory. Johann Gregorius Höroldt (1696 – 1775), a Viennese wallpaper painter, was hired as manager in the 1720s. He developed 16 new enamel paints which are still the basic paints for porcelain decoration today. Höroldt's contributions made Meissen a leader of polychrome enamel painting. He also developed the classic Meissen style which was to become the hallmark of Meissen's decoration. Höroldt was particularly known for his imaginative scenes of Chinese and Japanese life.

The 24-year-old court sculptor Johann Joachim Kaendler (1706 – 1775) was brought into the manufactory in 1730. Kaendler was born in 1706 at Fischbach, near Dresden, where his father was pastor. At age 17 he became an apprentice to the court sculptor, Benjamin Thomas, to work on the wood carvings in the Green Vault in the Dresden castle.

Augustus II ordered Kaendler to work on his pet project — the Japanese Palace. Augustus II had bought a small palace in 1717 across the Elbe River from his Dresden residence which he called the Japanese Palace. He gave orders to the manufactory for many pieces of porcelain to be displayed in his palace, particularly large, almost life-size animals and birds.

Kaendler started working with sculptor Johann Gottlieb Kirchner to complete a great number of large animals for the palace. Kaendler's talent in carving wood contributed to his success in porcelain modeling. He was a leading modeler for Meissen from 1735 – 1756. He had an acute observation of nature and was adaptable to new tasks. He had a keen artistic sense and an appreciation of current styles; therefore, he was able to interpret the strong Baroque style in the early eighteenth century and later the lightness and gaiety of the Rococo style. Kaendler produced thousands of models in his 43 years at Meissen and was responsible for the triumph of Meissen. For over 50 years the porcelain produced was unsurpassed by that of any other country. It was truly the Golden Age of Meissen.

VÉRITABLE EXTRAIT DE VIANDE LIEBIG.

Histoire de la Porcelaine — 4.
La porcelaine de Meissen (Saxe) apparaît pour la première fois à la foire de Pâques à Leipzig, en 1710.

"Meissen exhibited their early wares at the Leipzig Fair in 1710." (French trade card)

Early Accomplishments

INFLUENCE OF NEW BEVERAGES

The discovery of new drinks, tea, coffee, and chocolate changed the way of life in Europe and caused a demand for drinking vessels. Some of the first articles to be produced at the Meissen manufactory were breakfast sets consisting of six cups and saucers, a slop bowl, teapot, coffeepot, tea caddy, and sugar bowl. Jugs for chocolate, cream, or milk were made after 1730.

Highly decorated demitasse sets were commissioned as gifts for family members of royalty, members of the royal court, and foreign monarchs. The porcelain produced was richly decorated in multicolored overglaze painting and delicately modeled details.

UNDERGLAZE BLUE

The lovely tea ware decorated in underglaze blue, brought over by the East India Company to Europe from China in the seventeenth century was immediately successful. By the eighteenth century the demand for Chinese export porcelain became widespread. Augustus II ordered his new manufactory to produce blue underglaze decoration just like that on the Chinese porcelain he favored. Despite many trials, Böttger was not able to produce a usable paint for underglaze blue. In 1717 David Köhler developed the first usable blue paint that remained blue even at high temperatures. From 1739 the cobalt blue underglaze color had grown relatively free of problems, and the highly popular Blue Onion pattern (Zwiebelmuster) was developed. This pattern was based on a Chinese pattern from the Ming Dynasty and got its name from a stylized peach that resembled an onion. This became one of Meissen's most enduring patterns. More that 60 European and Oriental companies copied this decoration.

FAMOUS DINNER SERVICES

Augustus II died in 1733. His son and successor, Prince-Elector Friedrich August III (1696 – 1763) became King of Poland as Augustus III in October 1733. He did not share his father's enthusiasm for porcelain, but the Prime Minister of Saxony and Poland and new head of the Meissen manufactory, Heinrich Count von Brühl (1700 – 1763), did. As a supervisor of Meissen, Brühl could order porcelain for his own use free of charge.

One of the most elaborate early dinnerware sets was the Swan Service ordered by Count Brühl. It was first mentioned by Meissen in records dating May 1736, "A table service of entirely new design has been ordered by his Excellency, Minister Heinrich Count von Brühl."

The Swan Service (Schwansenservice) was modeled by Kaendler and Johann Eberlein. It was modeled and painted with aquatic motifs in the Rococo style. It included 2,000 pieces, and the entire surface was modeled in low relief.

Another magnificent service was ordered by Joseph Alexander Count von Sulkowski in 1735 with a wickerwork border. The main motif was a lion bearing a coat of arms. The set included massive tureens, candelabra, and sauceboats with curling feet and mask handles.

No. 459; Swans and Cupids; 4 Designs; $6.00 per M.

Swans and Cupids, early card.

Disastrous Seven Years' War

Meissen did not have any serious competition until 1756. Then came the devastating Seven Years' War when Meissen was occupied by Frederick the Great of Prussia, who started his own porcelain factory in Berlin. Many gifted artists were induced to leave Meissen's factory.

During the war, conditions were stressful in the manufactory. Much white porcelain left the factory to be painted by hausmalers. Hausmalers were freelance artists who decorated ceramics in their own studio or at home in the seventeenth century in Germany and Austria. The great dealer and politician Schimmelman bought and sold warehouses of Meissen porcelain — colored, white, and greenware — with the approval of King Frederick of Prussia after the Seven Years' War, apparently for services rendered to the Prussian army. This is how so much porcelain made its way to the studios of independent decorators, especially in Paris.

After the war ended in 1763, Augustus III returned to Dresden and tried to revitalize the factory. C. W. E. Dietrich was made a supervisor, and the Academic period began, which was characterized by the Neoclassical style. The Meissen company had economic problems because of foreign competition and protectionist policies. Some countries added import taxes while others actually prohibited the importation of Meissen wares. In 1760 English potter Josiah Wedgwood produced the first commercially successful earthenware which was pale enough to resemble porcelain. It was called creamware and instantly became popular worldwide, thus further hurting Meissen's sales.

Revival Under Marcolini

Camillo Count Marcolini was director of Meissen beginning in 1774. Under him there was a great revival of interest in Meissen. It is easy to recognize porcelain produced during his leadership, since the count decreed that a small star be placed under the crossed swords symbol.

One of Marcolini's most talented artists was the French sculptor and modeler Michel Victor Acier (1736 – 1799) who worked in the manufactory from 1764 to 1780. Acier and Kaendler worked together to complete the "Grand Russia Order," a set of tableware consisting of 40 groups and individual figures which had been ordered by Catherine II. Acier introduced many figures that were to become popular in the nineteenth century, such as children, lovers, musicians, gallants, gardeners, and cupids with mottos.

During the Marcolini period, there was increased production of common ware often decorated in underglaze blue. Even this common ware for everyday use was above average in body, potting, and painting.

The Nineteenth Century: Changing Times

Economic Upheaval

Foreign competition and protectionist policies weakened Meissen to such a degree that Count Marcolini asked to be released from his post. He died in 1814, and the company endured hard times.

By 1813 Meissen had been reduced to a disorganized, poorly administered company with low morale among its employees. Sales were so poor that the manufactory was reduced to making undecorated pieces to be sold to hausmalers and outside decorators.

One problem was the lowering of the quality standard. The manufactory produced large quantities of a low grade paste. Contaminated kaolin had been delivered to Meissen several times since 1812. The whole paste supply for 1814 was spoiled, and the porcelain that came out of the kiln was yellowish or gray.

Equipment and working techniques had become obsolete. Artistic development had not kept up with changing times.

Napoleon's devastating invasions from 1814 to 1833 brought poverty to the Germans, and there was little use or money for luxury goods. The transport of porcelain around Europe was almost impossible. Meissen resorted to making imitations of designs and materials made by Wedgwood, such as their Jasperware line. This was unsuccessful. Many earlier works were reproduced, such as Watteau style services. Colors were often ill matched to the designs. In 1827 porcelain was decorated by transfer printing under the glaze. In 1831 some tea and coffee sets were made from casts of cut glass but were not practical or successful. In the mid-eighteenth century

Meissen produced a large number of bisque busts and figure groups. These never achieved the beauty of the French and English biscuit porcelains. Old molds were brought out and used indiscriminately. Because so many of the old styles were reproduced, Meissen wares attracted unfavorable criticism at the 1845 Dresden Exhibit.

Economic Revival

Heinrich Gottlob Kühn became director from 1833 to 1870. Because of his energy and efforts, the manufactory was saved from bankruptcy and ruin. Kühn was forced to make long overdue technical and business reforms. One of his first successes was ending the system where an arcanist could hide the details of the paste from factory management. Thus it became easier for more people to research and experiment in the production of porcelain.

The most gifted artist under Kühn was Georg Friedrich Kersting (1785 – 1847). He designed the decoration for an elaborate table service presented to the Duke of Wellington. It had hand-painted and gilt English scenes.

A strong line of wares was produced for the London Exhibition in 1862. From the late 1870s Meissen began a solid trading base in the American market. There was a new demand from customers from England for old Rococo figures and decorative pieces.

Move and Expansion

Heinrich Kühn was also a leader of technical innovations. While he was director, the manufactory was moved to a new building in the Triebischtal Valley as there was no more room for expansion in the Albrechtsburg fortress. The foundation was laid in 1861, and the move was completed in 1865. The new building consisted of four wings around a rectangular yard. Round or multi-tier kilns were installed. The manufactory changed from wood to coal as the main fuel. In 1884 a mixing machine was installed, and the buildings were extended. The number of kilns was increased from four to seven.

Utilitarian Ware

Due to the Industrial Revolution in the late nineteenth century and the emergence of the new middle class, there was a considerable demand for reasonably priced porcelain dinnerware and decorative pieces. Ordinary items painted in blue underglaze became very popular, especially the Blue Onion pattern. By the 1870s this pattern was adapted to fit nearly every shape produced by the Meissen factory. China painting at home became quite popular, and Meissen made white blanks which helped supply the market.

The Twentieth Century: Talented Artists

Promising Artistic Development

Max Adolf Pfeiffer (1875 – 1957) was director of the manufactory from 1918 to 1933. His greatest contribution was to bring artistic standards to the highest level. He had a winning personality and attracted numerous artists, some working on a freelance basis.

Paul Scheurich (1883 – 1945) ranks first among the artists during the early twentieth century. He mastered the artistic expressiveness of porcelain and created figures and groups resembling the creations of Kaendler, but his interpretations were in tune with the twentieth century. He made more than 100 models, including figures, vases, and jars. His sculptures of the Russian Ballet Series were awarded a Grand Prix at the 1937 World Exhibition in Paris.

Another highly productive and original modeler was Emil Paul Börner (1888 – 1970). Börner started with the company in 1910 and designed dinner services, decorative pieces, and figures which have become standard parts of the manufactory's inventory. One of his greatest achievements was to design the first tunable porcelain bells which were first used in the Church of Our Lady in Meissen in 1929.

Professor Emil Börner and his tunable bells. German postcard. Kunstverlag Reinhard Rothe (F. Muhlbach), Meissen, R29256.

Erich Oskar Hösel (1869 – 1953) began with the manufactory in 1903 and was appointed design director in 1912. He and a team of capable workers devoted themselves to animal sculptures. One of them, Max Esser (1885 – 1943), was a freelance artist who modeled animals in lively movements. His Seagull on the Wave has become famous.

World War II

When the Nazi dictatorship began in 1933, Meissen's promising development ceased. Pfeiffer was discharged by the Nazis. The company continued to operate for a while producing war goods. In 1944 it was determined that the manufactory was unimportant to the war effort. In the summer of 1944, the removal of porcelain from the exhibition halls into the cellars of the Albrechtsburg was completed.

Meissen remained undamaged until the last year of World War II. At the end of April 1945 the Eastern Front had reached the northeast part of the town of Meissen. A number of the buildings were destroyed by artillery fire. Normal work was impossible, and production stopped. On May 15, 1945, Herbert Neuhaus was appointed director of the manufactory. Production slowly resumed in the autumn of 1945. In a radio broadcast at that time, Neuhaus said, "We shall go on, even if we have to prepare the clay with our bare hands." The manufactory's buildings and installations were repaired and expanded despite great difficulties.

Postwar — Difficult Times

After World War II Germany was split into four sections. The city of Meissen fell into the territory occupied by the Soviet Union. As part of war retribution, all of the Meissen industrial equipment, except the kilns, was shipped to Russia. In 1950 the factory operations were handed over to the newly formed German Democratic Republic. The quality of dinnerware suffered during the Russian influence. The German people had a tough struggle and were primarily concerned with putting food on the table instead of worrying about their dinnerware. As a result, Meissen developed a number of inexpensive and simple dinnerware lines after 1950 — plain white or with an inexpensive mechanical decoration. The quality did not always meet usual standards.

Decision on Future Goals

In the 1960s the manufactory had to make a decision. Was Meissen's future in the mass production of goods or was it to continue to do everything by hand, beginning with molding and continuing with the last stroke of the paint brush? Meissen decided on the latter; everything would be done by hand. The porcelain would continue to be rare and expensive, and no two pieces would be alike.

Artistic Development Team

In 1960, on the 250th anniversary of Meissen, the artistic development team was formed, headed by Ludwig Zepner and including Heinz Werner, Rudi Stolle, Volkmar Bretschneider, and Peter Strang. This group celebrated its first success with the Münchhausen dinner service in 1964 and the Arabian Nights in 1967.

Ludwig Zepner's most remarkable creation, dominating the manufactory of present day Meissen porcelain, has been the new shape for the tableware set — Large Cutout. Zepner sought inspiration from experiences in nature to design dinner, coffee, tea, and demitasse sets. Freely fashioned flowers and leaves provided the tableware sets with clear-cut outlines, gentle lines, and base and handle sections flowing out of the form. The sets were painted with ten newly developed patterns.

Heinz Werner's minute details and large area paintings have become known as the Werner style. Full of original ideas, he created the delightful patterns Münchhausen, Arabian Nights, and scenes from Shakespeare's *A Midsummer Night's Dream*.

Peter Strang was very innovative and daring, freely producing unique and amusing sculptures. He created figures from H. Werner's Arabian Nights and scenes from *A Midsummer Night's Dream*.

Meissen Today

Today Meissen's workforce has 1,100 employees, including 600 porcelain painters and sculptors. There are also 69 apprentices. The manufactory has 10,000 original and proprietary colors and 4,000 patterns. There are 150,000 tableware items, gifts, and figures in its inventory.

Meissen's present porcelain manufacturing philosophy is:

"Beautiful forms combined with skilled handicraft techniques acquired in years of training guarantee the high artistic value of Meissen porcelain. The diversity of patterns, strictly guarded formulas for colors and thousands of forms offer an inexhaustible selection for the collector and lover of porcelain.

These are prerequisites which those who love our porcelains value highly. The collector can always be certain that values which have come down over the centuries still apply. This is an obligation based on tradition, preserving one's unique character and the essential — one's characteristic style. This is why each piece of Meissen porcelain is an irreplaceable work of art which bestows upon each room and each table set its individual touch."

Main entrance of Meissen factory.

Meissen factory buildings.

Plaques at main entrance of Meissen factory.

Meissen porcelain has retained its value over time, and special pieces consistently reach high prices at international auctions. Part of this is because no two pieces are ever exactly alike. Almost all early eighteenth century Meissen is rare and valuable. Collectors are not likely to come across eighteenth century pieces except in museums or special auctions. Nineteenth and twentieth century pieces are readily available in the marketplace.

In her June 1997 article "19th Century Meissen" in *Antiques & Collecting*, Ute Ballay says, "Over the last few years nineteenth century Meissen has been one of the hottest areas of the ceramics market — often even out-performing earlier wares."

Michigan antique dealer Joe Delgiudice says, "Meissen is so hot right now I have difficulty getting enough quality items for customers. The stampede is coming from Japan and Germany, and it just gets even busier during the holidays." ("Make Mine Meissen," by Chriss Swaney, *Antique Trader*, 12/18/2002)

Meissen has had its proud, prosperous days and its periods of low morale and economic decline. It has weathered wars, depressions, loss of royal support, and many other problems. Today it rightly deserves international fame for outstanding production over its long and unique history.

Meissen Drawing School

The professional education of young artists has long been a tradition at the Meissen manufactory. Höroldt trained talented students in a six-year apprenticeship in 1724, and Kaendler provided regular training in 1740.

The Drawing School was established in 1764 as a branch of the Dresden Art Academy founded in the same year. This school has been the first and most important stage of the education of gifted students in the field of porcelain decoration. The school celebrated its 225th anniversary in 1989 and is the oldest educational institution of the ceramics industry in Europe. Today most Meissen porcelain painters, sculptors, and modelers are graduates of the Dresden Art Academy.

Meissen also has an excellent in-house school of its own. It provides a one- to three-year course of study to teach its own distinctive style of painting. Meissen also offers special painting and creativity seminars for the general public. These are taught by experienced instructors from the manufactory.

Exhibition Hall

Meissen Director Julius Heintz (1846 – 1931) had a special building constructed alongside the Meissen manufactory between 1912 and 1915. The purpose was to show part of Meissen's vast porcelain collection to the public. It was a museum, as well as a sales tool, and it provided artists with an opportunity for study.

The architects created a building in a combination Neoclassic and Art Nouveau style. It was called the Model Hall and was opened to the public on January 1, 1916. It was later named the China Museum in 1960 and is now called the Exhibition Hall. About 3,000 items from Meissen's collection are selected each year for display at the hall. On the first floor, there is a festival hall with a large dinner table for 12 people, decorated each year with changing dinner sets. On the second floor there is a dome covered room with a ceiling painting by Professor Achtenhagen, done in 1915.

The hall also holds a demonstration workshop with four work stations. An explanation of the demonstrations is available on tape in 25 languages. The Exhibition Hall is open to the public April 1 to October 31, every day except Monday from 8 a.m. to 4:30 p.m. Over 300,000 visitors from Germany and abroad visit each year.

Elaborate figural military group in Meissen Museum.

Meissen Exhibition Hall (postcard Bild und Heimat-Reichenbach Vogth).

Gründung der ersten europäischen Porzellanmanufaktur 1710

Display in showroom, History of Meissen Works.

The Manufacturing Process

The manufacturing process can be divided into four main parts: preparation of the raw materials, shaping the item, firing, and decorating.

Raw Material

Most antique dealers and collectors of Meissen porcelain know why it is so special. It starts with the clay. About seven and one-half miles from the Meissen manufactory, hidden away on a birch covered hillside, is Europe's smallest mine located at Seilitz. It is here that miners work for Meissen extracting kaolin, which is 65% of the raw materials used in making porcelain. The clay, which is exceptionally white and iron-free, is brought to the surface in small carts as it has been for the past 225 years. One of the reasons Meissen porcelain has remained superior is due to its plasticity and very high content of kaolin.

The kaolin is mixed with quartz and feldspar through various processes to insure it is pure. The more kaolin, the harder the porcelain. Quartz is a non-plastic mineral that decreases the plasticity of a porcelain. It also aids in the vitrification of porcelain in the kiln.

Feldspar is a mineral that softens in temperatures above 1150°C but does not run. It is feldspar that contributes to the density and stability of Meissen porcelain. The Chinese called kaolin the flesh and feldspar the bones of porcelain.

The precise mixture of the ingredients varies according to the object being made. Although the recipe for porcelain, once the carefully guarded secret of the Meissen manufactory, is now widely known, Meissen porcelain is still unique. It is harder, whiter, and more translucent that that made by other porcelain manufactories. The materials used by Meissen have always had to meet various standards, such as strength, pliability, and plasticity for making figurines. The formula of the ingredients has remained almost constant up to the present time.

Preparing

When the proper mixture is achieved, the ingredients are mixed together. Water is then pressed out of the creamy liquid, which results in a workable clay that can be stored for up to a year until it is needed.

The clay can either be thrown on a potter's wheel or put in a mold. Since the method of placing the clay on a potter's wheel is not conducive to mass production, molding is used at the Meissen manufactory. This method is ideal for long production runs of objects which have to be identical in size and shape, such as a dinnerware service or a cup and saucer. A porcelain figure is made from a number of molds.

Designing and Modeling

The first step in creating a new shape is for the designer to make a drawing of the design to be used in production. Then a modeler makes a clay model of the item. Meissen molds are exact copies in reverse of the original model. These molds are working molds and require great skill. Meissen considers model and mold making to be one of the most important parts of the production process. From these working molds, the master molds for production are made.

Casting

Several different methods of casting, such as core casting, hollow casting, or a combination of both may be used due to the different configurations of the item to be produced. Casting is done from slip which is made by adding purified water to the powdered mixture of kaolin, feldspar, and quartz. This slip has the consistency of heavy cream. After all impurities are removed, the slip is poured into a mold. The dry mold absorbs the moisture from the slip, and the excess is poured off. When the piece comes out of the mold, a finisher smoothes the item and eliminates all mold seams with a soft wet sponge.

Depending on the nature of the item to be made, the process changes accordingly. For instance, a molded plate would need very little, if any, assembly, but figures would have to be cut into many pieces and molded separately and then put together without any trace of mold seams. When this has been accomplished, the item is ready for the kiln.

The making of a cup in a plaster mold at the Meissen demonstation studio.

Firing

During the firing in the kiln an item goes through many chemical changes. The heat in the kiln makes the kaolin fuse with all the other ingredients into a new composition that has physical properties very different from those of the raw materials. It is now called biscuit or greenware and has a leatherlike consistency. Today the kilns at Meissen are gas-heated and do not require any protective enclosures for the porcelain. They are called batch kilns and have centrally controlled temperatures. After firing at 1450°C, the resulting product is genuine porcelain. Meissen makes the highest grade product in the field of ceramics. It is hard, white, fine-textured, and translucent. It lends itself to many artistic and utilitarian purposes.

Checking the condition of the mold.

Glazing

The next step protects the bisque piece with a transparent glaze. This glaze gives a brilliant surface to the porcelain. The glaze mixture is mostly quartz and limestone. Glazing is done by dipping a piece in the glaze solution or airbrushing with a spray gun. It appears as a white coating which, as a result of being fired, becomes transparent and forms a protective glass-like coat over the piece, thoroughly sealing the object. The piece is then fired again. It takes one to three days for it to cool.

Porcelain glazes were changed more often than porcelain paste. Glazes not only have to match the physical properties of the paste, but they also have to fuse with the paste during the firing and cool down at the same speed without creating tensions, which could result in fine fissures or crazing. After the cooling of a piece is achieved, it is ready to be decorated.

Decorating

In general there are two ways of decorating porcelain. The first method applies to the plastic decorations on the rough unfused body of the piece itself in the form of reliefs, perforations, embossing, or simply by impressing or engraving. The second is accomplished by coloring or gilding. Colors are applied either under the glaze after the first firing or over the glaze following the second firing. The difference is that under the glaze paints must be able to stand the high temperature of the heat in the kiln, while painting over the glaze requires a much lower heat.

After the item is decorated, gold is applied if required, and the item is fired again. After the gold is fired, it is ready for a final hand polishing.

Inspecting

The practice at Meissen is to inspect every piece after every step of its production. Because of computer controlled kilns today, there are very few defects found on a piece of porcelain. These are sold at the factory shop for 20% less.

At Meissen chemists, modelers, designers, painters, and skilled technicians are thoroughly trained in the basic principles of the craft of porcelain manufacturing. Classes are given for fine-tuning skills, and many employees have to serve years as apprentices under the watchful eyes of master supervisors. Meissen places a high premium on expert workmanship. A well organized, highly trained group of artists and craftsmen are necessary to produce Meissen's high quality porcelain.

A finished cup in greenware stage.

European Decorative Styles

1710 – 1740 Baroque Style

The Baroque style is characterized by massive form and vigorous movement. Heavily ornamented tableware and decorative pieces were enriched with vivid ground colors.

1735 – 1775 Rococo Style

French in origin, this style is characterized by light, graceful designs and fanciful forms. Handles have curves and scrolls. Fruits and flowers are strewn all over in a light and delicate manner.

1775 – 1820 Empire or Neoclassical Style

This French style originated during the reign of Napoleon and is characterized by straight lines and symmetry. Influenced by archaeological discoveries in Pompeii in the 1770s, the decoration of the ancient Greeks and Romans became fashionable during this period.

1820 – 1890 Rococo Revival

This style is characterized by light, graceful design, fanciful forms, and a profusion of shells, flowers, foliage, and fruits. Handles had curves and c-scrolls.

1890 – 1910 Jugendstil

A German term meaning "Youth Style," in France it was called the Art Nouveau movement for "New Art." It was characterized by sensuous female figures and flowers and leaves in undulating lines, often with flowing vines.

Popular Shapes

Shape 01 Old Ozier (Alt Ozier)

This shape was created by Kaendler and his assistant Eberlein in 1736. Ozier refers to the willow twigs used in wicker work. A Rococo variation, New Ozier shape, was created in the 1740s.

Shape 02 Neubrandenstein

In 1744 J. F. Eberlein created this shape for Friedrich August von Brandenstein, master of the kitchen at the noble court of Dresden. This graceful shape has a lattice relief at the rim and curved, wave-like lines on the body, typical of the Rococo period.

Shape 00 New Cutout (Never Ausschnitt)

This shape was created by J. Kaendler in 1745, and it became the manufactory's most widely used shape for many of its patterns. It is plain except for the wavy edge cut.

Shape 03 Neumaiseille

This shape was developed by J. Kaendler in 1739. It features floral elements and cartouches in relief around a smooth center. This shape lends itself to Watteau scenes, floral decoration, and chinoiseries.

SHAPE 05 SWAN SERVICE

This shape was a result of a six-year effort by J. Kaendler from 1735 to 1741. An intricate relief of waves of flowing water, dominated by swans gliding through reeds among herons and fish were carved into the porcelain. It symbolized the ebb  and flow of life itself. Today this shape has little additional decoration other than strewn flowers or just a white ground with a simple gold edge and border.

SHAPE 17 FORM X

This shape was designed during the second half of the nineteenth century. It lends itself to gold ornamentation in lavish gold bronze and gold lines. A characteristic of this shape is the vine leaves in relief with decoration on the base of each item.

SHAPE 08 GOTZKOSWKY RELIEF

This shape was developed in 1741 for J. Ernst Gotzkoswky (1710 – 1775), a Berlin merchant who was a good customer of Meissen. This shape takes the form of a radial flower garland with eight sections. Four of these parts are decorated with relief flowers, and four are plain, to hold painted flowers. This shape is well suited to camaieu painting (one color), especially copper-green Watteau paintings.

SHAPE 23
LARGE CUTOUT
(GROSSER AUSSCHNITT)

In the early 1970s Ludwig Zepner, head of Meissen's design department, developed this romantic design. The bases and handles flow gracefully out of the form. Plates, saucers, and lids resemble the leaves of water lilies.

SHAPE 15 FORM B

This shape was created in 1855 by Ernst August Leuteritz, head of the design department. It is a richly ornamental shape with gold bronze. In addition to white, the most popular ground color for this shape is cobalt blue because of the dramatic contrast with the white and gold.

SHAPE 28 WAVES
(WELLENSPIEL)

This is a new shape created for the twenty-first century to embody today's elegance. It was inspired by the movement of gentle breezes on the ponds around the manufactory.

SHAPE 29
WAVES RELIEF

Also created in the twenty-first century, this shape is characterized by images of waves rippling across a pond recreated in relief.

Marks

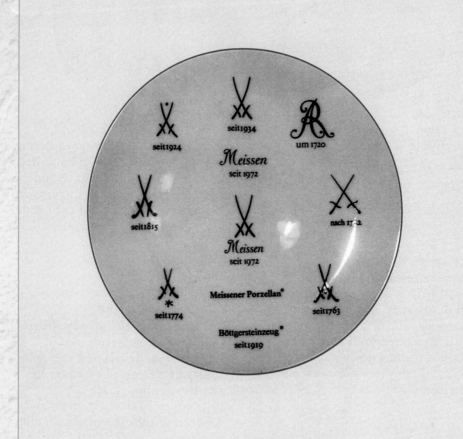

Crossed Swords Mark

The trademark of Meissen, the crossed swords, is probably the oldest and best known of all the porcelain marks used. On November 8, 1722, manufactory inspector Johann Melchior Steinbruck came up with the idea to mark Meissen porcelain with the Elector's swords: "...Therefore, I would prefer a mark related to the Saxon Electoral coat-of-arms, for instance, the Electoral swords, so that other nations might recognize that the wares so signed were manufactured in the Electorate of Saxony."

(Verlag, R. V. Meiben & Meissen)

Steinbruck's idea was approved, and since 1723 the sword mark has been painted underglaze on each piece in a cobalt blue color. It is always painted by hand after the first firing and is referred to as "swording." The mark is protected by the glazing and second firing. In the course of time, the sword mark has undergone changes, and it differs from piece to piece because it is applied by hand by different painters.

Rare Augustus Rex mark used for the Polish-Saxon rulers Augustus II and Augustus III from 1720.

Letters stand for Meissner Porzellan-Manufaktur, used in 1722.

Letters stand for Königliche Porzellan-Manufaktur, used for painted articles after December 1722.

Marks of pseudo-Chinese appearance used particularly for exports to Turkey. This is known as Aesculap rod, whip mark, or Mercurus rod, 1720 – 1730.

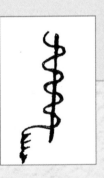

1725 – 1763.

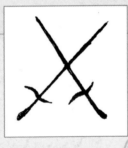

1723 – 1725.

Academic or Dot period, 1763 – 1774.

Marcolini period, 1774 – 1817.

At the end of the Marcolini period Meissen was in financial trouble. In order to cut production costs, a cheaper grade of porcelain was used. This mark means regular paste, 1817 – 1824.

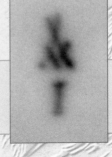

Cheaper paste, 1817 – 1824.

After 1824, a period began when crossed swords were painted carelessly, 1824 – 1850.

On the swords, the pommels were emphasized by a little knob. This mark showed a distinct curve of the hilts with pommels on the outside, 1850 – 1924.

Two hundred year anniversary mark, June 6, 1910 – June 5, 1911.

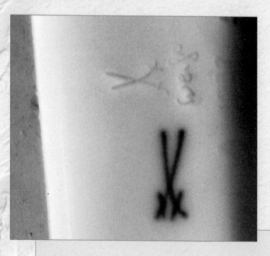

Mark for articles that are supposed to be sold white; mark is impressed, 1915 – present.

Max Adolph Pfeiffer introduced a new mark with slightly curved symmetrical blades with a dot between the tips, 1924 – 1934.

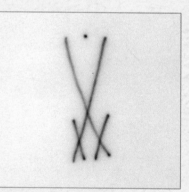

Special mark to commemorate 1000 years since the founding of the Albrechtsburg castle, 1929.

In 1933 Pfeiffer was forced to resign by the Nazis, and the dot was eliminated from the mark the following year. After that the shape of the crossed swords as designed under Pfeiffer was retained and is still in use today, 1934 – present.

After the Soviet Union handed Meissen to the government of the GDR in 1950, the new administration introduced additions to the mark to identify the period of production. These additions appear in blue paint under the glaze near the footring.

A smaller arc below the hilts was used after World War II to symbolize the hope for peace among antagonistic nations, 1945 – 1946.

Numbering System

Meissen did not always have a consistent or accurate numbering system. Robert E. Röntgen puts some order into Meissen's complex numbering system and explains it in detail in *The Book of Meissen*.

Figures and groups often have model numbers incised into the porcelain at the base:

1765 – 1850, A1 – Z100
1850 – 1910, A101 – Z200

In 1910 a new series was started beginning with A201 and proceeding to A300, then B201 – B300 and so on, ending with X in 1973. After this, a new system was developed with about three different sets of numbers on each figure.

Cancellation or Incised Marks

Many Meissen items found in the marketplace show the crossed swords with incising. Their meaning has been interpreted differently by authors and dealers. Röntgen, in *The Book of Meissen* says, "Any attempt to find a logical system for the different kinds of incisions is futile." In his book, Röntgen does try to make some sense of the marks and their meaning. Here are a few of the more frequent marks found on pieces today.

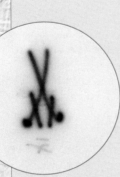

Single incised line usually indicating the piece was sold in white, and decoration was done outside the factory.

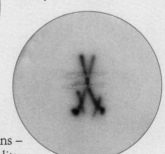

Two incisions – second quality.

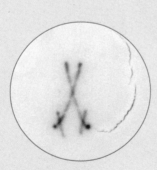

Three incisions – inferior quality.

Four incisions – brac.

Ornate and beautifully hand painted, Meissen decorative ware is porcelain at its finest. Meissen calls these special pieces fancy ware, and today they make up 25% of the company's production.

Motifs

Meissen used a variety of motifs on its decorative ware. Some are as popular with collectors today as they were in the eighteenth century.

Birds

Through the ages, birds have amused and enchanted their owners with their intelligence, beautiful colors, and ability to mimic the human voice. From the beginning, the bird was an extremely popular subject at the Meissen manufactory. At the request of the Saxon Court, one of the earliest classical tableware designs was decorated with nicely painted native birds. Towards the end of the eighteenth century, bird designs were increasingly in demand. The public showed a preference for colorful, naturalistically painted birds above all other motifs.

Swans were used frequently as a decorative theme at the manufactory. In Roman mythology the swan was an exceptional creature into which the gods could transform themselves. Jupiter changed himself into a handsome swan and was able to make Leda fall in love with him. Meissen's magnificent Swan service is one of the most famous dinnerware services of all time.

Bird and butterfly in flowering tree, 1918 postcard.

Family of swans, German postcard,
M. Ettlinger & Co., London.

"Some say they don't believe
That Angels can be seen or heard.
What a shame such blindness
What a pity such deafness
When the Song of songs abounds...
And Heaven's flyers are all around...
Only thinly disguised...as birds."

INTERNET:
HTTP://WWW.PETSTATION.COM/BIRDS.HTML

The Swan service was completed in 1742 and consisted of 2,000 pieces. Its central motif was rough water which symbolized the eternal flow of life. The surface of each piece had a fine relief of waves. Although the swan was the dominant motif, there were sea animals and plants living in the water, such as herons and reeds. The set included table figures and elaborate figural centerpieces. One of the best decorative elements, the two swans shown facing in profile in low relief in the center of a plate, came from an engraving by Wenceslaus Hollar. Applied figures were on lids and sides of serving items. The lid of a sugar bowl might have three nymphs winding a garland around the neck of a swan.

The Swan service was originally made for the Empress of Russia, but she thought it was too expensive and decided not to take it. Count Brühl adopted the service for himself and had his coat-of-arms painted on it.

Hunting

Hunting was the center of life at European courts in the eighteenth century and became a favorite subject of Meissen paintings. Notable hunting experiences were memorialized on porcelain. One of the best known designs was the New Cutout developed by Johann Kaendler. His representation of the hunt was very realistic. He skillfully united people and animals in groups full of movement.

The Large Cutout service, designed by Ludwig Zepner in the 1970s, was a combination of under and overglaze paintings of forest and hunting scenes and was taken from the old designs. The Large Cutout is one of Meissen's top sales leaders today.

Watteau Courting Scenes

Watteau paintings portray figures, usually a man and woman, in a landscape or garden setting. These decorations were copied from originals by eighteenth century French artists, such as François Boucher, Johannes Ridinger, Philips Wouvermen, and Antoine Watteau.

Jean Antoine Watteau (1684 – 1721) was a French Rococo artist whose charming graceful paintings show his interest in the theatre and ballet. He is best known for his fetes gallante, which are small romantic landscapes with wistful lovers in fancy dress. A set of copperplate engravings by Watteau was purchased by the factory in 1741.

Large dinnerware services were completed with the new Watteau paintings, often in copper green. Couples were cuddling, playing music, or relaxing in a garden. These little scenes were surrounded by embossed flowers.

Man and woman in eighteenth century costume, 1916. Italian postcard, UFF Pev. Stampa, Milano, signed M. Faris.

A Watteau service was made for Princess Maria Amalia Christene for her marriage to Karl IV of Naples in 1743. In 1745 Meissen made green services in the Watteau style for the Empress Elisabeth of Russia. There are also tete-a-tete sets, solitaires, and snuff boxes ornamented with wonderful decorations inspired by Watteau and Boucher. The decoration required the highest degree of perfection and expertise.

The well-known Green Watteau service was made for the Saxon court and was first delivered in 1748. It remained popular during the time of Marcolini. The service was decorated from scenes from Watteau's engravings and included flowers. The painting was predominately in copper green and enamel colors.

Meissen coffee service, courting scenes designed by A. G. Eras (1835 – 1907) and E. A. Leuteritz (1818 – 1893). 1984 postcard, courtesy of Meissen.

Landscapes

Meissen painter Johann George Heintz was much admired for his outstanding European landscapes which were based on Dutch engravings. The style gained popularity in the 1730s and soon the painting of harbor scenes, landscapes, and battles achieved great popularity.

River or port scenes, with ships docked along the banks and merchants peddling their wares, are referred to as harbor scenes. They are tiny paintings with deep perspective. They were painted in Höroldt's studio as early as the mid-1720s. His scenes usually featured Chinese merchants which were changed to European merchants in the early 1730s.

Meissen artists began to transfer the paintings in the famous Semper Gallery in Dresden, Germany onto porcelain around 1800. Giovanni Antonio Canaletto (1697 – 1768) was an Italian painter known for his sparkling views of Venice, Dresden, and other cities in Europe and England. Meissen artists copied his topographical paintings on porcelain, and these items with city views are highly desirable today.

Meissen artist copying scene from canvas, 1984. Postcard of showroom, courtesy of Meissen.

Allegorical scene "La Danza d'Apollo con le Muse," by Giulio Romano. Early Cartolina postcard, Stengel & Co., Dresden.

Allegorical

Tales from Greek and Roman mythology were widely known in the eighteenth century. There were abundant classical statues in the gardens and parks in the Royal Palace as well as allegorical paintings. Kaendler had a solid background in the classical arts and was in his element when creating allegorical designs, especially cupids, on his decorative porcelain.

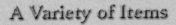

Portrait painting was often used as a method of decorating certain Meissen pieces such as vases, urns, plates, and cups. The face of a beautiful woman was a common subject, although famous men were often used as well, such as Augustus II and Napoleon. This type of decoration was very expensive to produce as it was only done by the top Meissen portrait artists. At the end of the eighteenth century there was an increased demand by the wealthy for portrait items. Johann George Loehnig (1745 – 1806) was a famous Meissen portrait painter.

Beautiful woman portrait painting by Asti, Raphael Tuck & Sons, Connoisseur 1906 postcard.

A Variety of Items

The variety of porcelain decorative items made at the Meissen manufactory was quite extraordinary. The most remarkable were the massive tableware services with the ornate serving pieces and figures. In 1745 Sir Charles Hanbery-Williams, English ambassador to the Polish court, wrote home about a dinner party given by Count Brühl for 200 people. He was amazed by a porcelain fountain at least eight feet high which was displayed in the center of the table when dessert was served.

Massive vases and centerpieces modeled with cupids, fruits, and flowers and decorated with Watteau figures were popular. Elaborate lids with sprigs of applied flowers were made. Compotes with frolicking cherubs and applied flowers were part of elaborate dessert sets. These services included 12 dessert plates, fruit bowls, compotes, and three-tier centerpieces often supported by figures.

Figural sweetmeat dishes were made in pairs and are popular with collectors today. They usually depicted a man and woman reclining on a dish. A rare important set of 27" ewers was designed in 1850, representing the four elements: water, fire, air, and earth.

Early tureens were quite elaborate, and many of the same forms are still being made today. The cover knob or finial often took the form of a cupid with a horn of plenty from which fruit or flowers poured out over the cover. Other decorative items made in the eighteenth and nineteenth centuries were clock cases, writing stands, bells, holy water pots, and dresser sets.

Meissen decorative urn with allegorical painting, Photograph from Meissen Museum.

Meissen figural clock, T. Helmig (1859 – 1939), 1984 postcard, courtesy of Meissen.

Chess sets have always been popular items at the Meissen manufactory. Augustus II was insistent in his demand for a chess set. The pieces were fashioned from white and red porcelain. Kings were clad in armor or Roman costumes. In the twentieth century Max Esser created three sets during his employment. The most unusual was his chess set called Sea World, first designed in the 1920s. On the board, the eyes of two huge octopi look at the game. The King and Queen are water lotuses, rooks are octopi, bishops are crabs, knights are seahorses, and pawns are starfish. The set was first painted in red and black with gold accents. Esser was inspired by the 1923 world chess champion José Raúl Capablanca from Cuba. A new edition came out in 1999 with a special Meissen sign as part of the limited edition century collection.

Chess set, Prof. Esser (1885 – 1943). 1984 postcard, courtesy of Meissen.

Decorative Techniques

From the beginning, evidence suggests that decoration on one piece was divided among several craftsmen. The manufactory had separate decorators for figures, landscapes, battle scenes, flowers, and birds. Another painter specialized in cartouches, and gilders did gold work. Even lines were the task of one artist listed as a line painter. Each piece might be worked on by four or five people. "This extremely modern process is one of the underlying reasons for the consistency of quality of Meissen decoration from the outset." (Morley-Fletcher, Hugo. *Antique Porcelain in Color*)

In 1831 Meissen began to copy many of the popular cut glass patterns of the day. This was abandoned by the end of the nineteenth century. Examples are scarce today.

Covered cups with portrait miniatures in royal blue were made at the manufactory around 1740. The cylindrical cup shape was frequently used in the Neoclassical period. Cups and pots with swan handles became important decorative shapes at Meissen. In the second half of the nineteenth century, Ernst August Leutertz created the snake handle vase which is still popular today. Cups and pots can be found with snake handles as well.

Many Meissen pieces have reticulation or piercing, usually on borders of plates and along rims and feet of vases and urns. The piercing is done when the piece is still in the greenware stage before biscuit firing. A reticulated piece is cut out by hand with a small knife. It takes more than an hour to cut out a simple pierced plate. For this reason Meissen's large openwork pieces, such as baskets, elaborately pierced centerpieces, and potpourri vase covers and stands are expensive and highly prized by collectors.

Decorative plate, c. 1850 – 1900, four incised marks. Pink swirled border, 11¼", small manufacturing bump on back of plate, cut glass motif, center medallion of hand-painted birds perched on a flowering tree. $450.00 – 500.00.

Close-up of birds.

Vase, c. 1850 – 1924. Bottle-shaped, 3"h, applied blue forget-me-nots on a vine. $275.00 – 300.00.

Bowl, c. 1950s, two incised marks, 10", cobalt and gilt leaves on border, hand-painted flowers in center. $400.00 – 450.00.

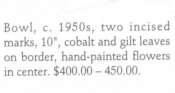

Close-up of snake handle.

Coffee cup and saucer, c. 1850 – 1870. Cup with snake handle with scales and gilded foot, 2¾"w x 3". Saucer with ⅓" gold band, 5⅞". Unusual nine-petal design with hand-painted bow at each point and a wreath with flowers. $900.00 – 950.00.

Close-up of pattern.

Coffee cup and saucer, c. 1870 – 1900. Can-shaped cup with square handle, 2½"w x 2½"h. Saucer, 5". Hand gilt work, rich cobalt blue ground with medallion of hand-painted flowers. $700.00 – 750.00.

Tray, c. 1860s. Square with two handles, 16", hand-painted flowers on white, cobalt and gold trim. $1,200.00 – 1,500.00.

Close-up of blue ribbon on handle.

Demitasse cup and saucer, c. 1930s. Cup with twisted handle with blue ribbon and six feet, applied and hand-painted flowers and gilt. $550.00 – 600.00.

Miniature teacup and saucer, c. 1850 – 1870. One incised mark, outside painting, round cup with loop handle, 1⅔"w x 1⅛"h. Saucer, 2⅔", hand-painted cupid in reserve in purple camaieu style on yellow ground. $300.00 – 350.00.

Demitasse cup and saucer, c. 1850 – 1924. Cup with swan handle, exquisite painting of exotic birds, swans, and butterflies, gilt clovers on border. $600.00 – 700.00.

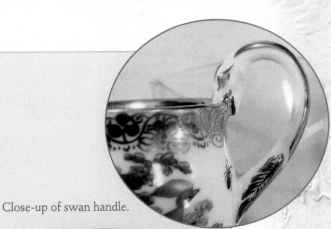

Close-up of swan handle.

Close-up of painting.

Close-up of cupid.

Tureen, c. 1850 – 1900, two incised marks. Neubrandenstein shape, 15" x 8½" x 12", applied cupid figure atop lid with a horn of plenty (end of thumb is off), blue flowers and blue flower handles. $800.00 – 900.00.

Close-up of handle.

Vase, c. 1850 – 1924. Two-part bolted vase with two entwined snake handles, 10¾", lush hand-painted flowers with purple trim. $800.00 – 900.00.

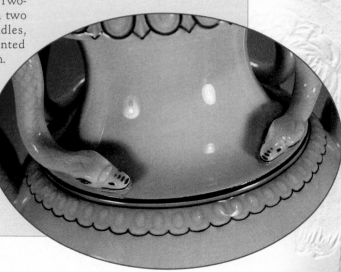

Close-up of snake handles.

Miniature cup and saucer, c. 1850 – 1924, two incised marks. Cup with loop handle, gilt decoration inside cup, hand-painted birds. $250.00 – 275.00.

Close-up of painting.

Tray, c. 1952. Large square tray with two ornate handles, 16", purple flowers and gilt. $900.00 – 1,000.00.

Close-up of fruit.

Fruit bowl, c. 1924 – 1934. 14" x 2", luscious array of hand-painted fruit in center, heavy gilt flowers and scrolls. $600.00 – 650.00.

Close-up of gilt flowers.

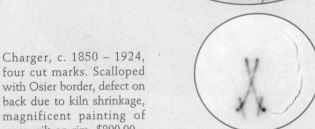

Close-up of flower painting.

Charger, c. 1850 – 1924, four cut marks. Scalloped with Osier border, defect on back due to kiln shrinkage, magnificent painting of roses, gilt on rim. $800.00 – 900.00.

Close-up of defect.

Covered bowl, c. 1850 – 1924. 5¼" x 4", applied flowers on bowl and lid. $450.00 – 500.00.

Another view of bowl.

Compote, c.1930s. Footed, scalloped, with gilt molded leaves on border, hand-painted flowers and gilt. $400.00 – 450.00.

Close-up of transfer.

Demitasse cup and saucer, c. 1850 – 1900, two incised marks. Bute-shaped cup with twisted branch handle, transfers of cupids and maidens in purple camieux. $100.00 – 150.00.

Close-up of flowers.

Charger, c. 1930s. Heavy gilt scrolls, 11",
hand-painted flowers. $400.00 – 450.00.

Close-up of gilding.

Inkwell set, c. 1860. Footed
covered inkwells and candle-
holder on 11½" x 6" tray,
applied flowers and gilt decoration. $5,000.00 – 5,500.00.

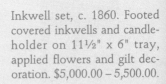

Another view of inkwell set.

Figural clock, c. 1890s. Four putti and base, 20½"h, applied flower decoration, part of three-piece garniture, see candleabra below. $13,000.00 – 14,000.00.

Teacup and saucer, c. 1850 – 1924, two incised marks. Quatrefoil shaped cup with pinched loop handle, seascape scenes alternating with flowers on gilt. $150.00 – 175.00.

Figural candelabrum, c. 1890s. Four holders, figure of girl holding basket, 18¼"h, part of three-piece garniture with above clock. $13,000.00 – 14,000.00.

Figural candelabrum, c. 1890s. Four holders, figure of boy holding plate, 18¼"h; part of three-piece garniture with above clock. $13,000.00 – 14,000.00.

Tete-a-tete set, c. 1890. Six-piece set including tray
(17" x 10"), teapot (7½"), creamer (3½"), covered
sugar (4½"), and two covered cups and saucers.
Sneeballan decoration, applied birds on lid
finials. $7,000.00 – 8,000.00.

One of a pair of figural candleholders,
c. 1820s. Boy atop dolphin on bed of
coral. 14"l x 9"w x 13¾"h, all white.
$11,000.00 – 12,000.00 for set.

Close-up of boy on dolphin.

One of a pair of figural candleholders,
c. 1820s. Boy atop dolphin on bed of
coral. 14"l x 9"w x 13¾"h, all white.
$11,000.00 – 12,000.00 for set.

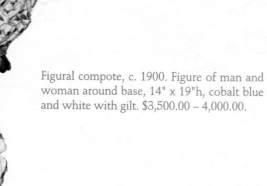

Figural compote, c. 1900. Figure of man and woman around base, 14" x 19"h, cobalt blue and white with gilt. $3,500.00 – 4,000.00.

Bell, c. 1850 – 1900. 4"h, topographical medallion of Schlefs Albrechtsburg on front, two floral medallions on back, cobalt with gilt decoration. $600.00 – 700.00.

Close-up of topographical medallion.

Back of bell.

Flowers on back.

Close-up of cameo.

Close-up of royal crest.

Coffee cup and saucer, c. 1817 – 1824. Footed cup with gilt inside, 2¾" x 3". Saucer, 5⅓". Cup with relief bisque portrait or cameo of King Frederick Augustus III, royal crest framed with laurel leaves on saucer. $1,000.00 – 1,200.00.

Close-up of strawberries inside gilded cartouche.

Decorative plate, c. 1850 – 1900. 9", hand-painted red grapes in center with strawberries, blueberries, and mushrooms in the gilt framed cartouches on border. $450.00 – 500.00.

Close-up of grapes.

Covered coffee cup and saucer, c. 1830 – 1850. Cup with twisted feather
handle, 3" x 2¼". Saucer, 5½", lid with flower finial; marbleized royal
blue ground, hand-painted scenes of men on horseback.
$700.00 – 800.00.

Close-up of
painting on lid of cup.

Close-up of
painting on saucer.

Another view showing handle.

Tureen, c. 1850 – 1900. Large, with feathered handles and cupid finial with cornucopia of fruit. 10¾" without the handles, 9"h, rich cobalt blue border with coat-of-arms with a deer or elk. $1,200.00 – 1,500.00.

Close-up of cupid.

Close-up of coat-of-arms.

Demitasse cup and saucer, c. 1924 – 1934. Cup in Royal Flute shape, scenic cartouche of four men playing a game on a red ground, gilt decoration. $300.00 – 350.00.

Close-up of scene.

Close-up of cupids.

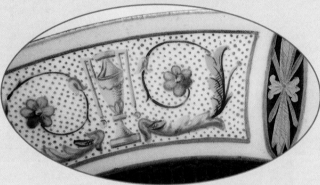

Close-up of coat-of-arms.

Plate, c. 1915 – 1919, painted outside factory, 9",
center medallion has three cupids, ornate border
with gilt urns, forget-me-nots, and gold dots.
$600.00 – 700.00.

Close-up of cupids.

Plate, c. 1850 – 1900. 8", floral cartouches in reticulated border,
hand-painted cupids holding grapes in center. $700.00 – 800.00.

Pot de crème, c. 1850 – 1924.
Lid with flower bud finial,
2½"w x 3½"h, hand-painted
bird, flowers, bugs, gilt.
$250.00 – 300.00.

Close-up of scene.

Charger, c. 1850 – 1900. 9¼", magnificent
allegorical scene. $3,000.00 – 3,500.00.

Close-up of scene.

Dish, c. 1930s, two incised marks. 5½", hand-painted bird with gilt. $150.00 – 200.00.

Close-up of bird.

Close-up of courting scene.

Demitasse cup and saucer, c. 1850 – 1900. Quatrefoil shaped cup, 3¼"w x 1¾". Saucer, 5⅛" x 5½", gilt flowers and scrolls inside and outside, rich cobalt ground with medallions of flowers on saucer and courting scene on cup. $575.00 – 600.00.

Coffee cup and saucer, c. 1850 – 1924. Cup in Royal Flute shape, Watteau painting with gilt. $300.00 – 350.00.

Close-up of courting scene.

Close-up of floral cartouche.

Plate, c. 1850 – 1900. Reticulated, 9", well-painted courting scene in center framed by gold decoration, floral cartouches on border, burgundy red ground. $600.00 – 700.00.

Close-up of well-painted courting scene.

Demitasse cup and saucer, c. 1850 – 1924. Quatrefoil shaped cup with Dresden handle, courting scene portraits on cup, floral medallions on saucer, gilt scrolls on cobalt. $550.00 – 650.00.

Close-up of courting scene on cup.

Close-up of scene.

Reticulated plate, c. 1850 – 1900. 9", three floral cartouches on reticulated border, cobalt ground with hand-painted courting scene in center framed by gold decoration. $500.00 – 600.00.

Shoe, c. 1850 – 1890. 3¾", royal blue ground with hand-painted courting scene on toe, gilt decoration. $400.00 – 450.00.

Close-up of courting scene.

Close-up of courting scene.

Bell, c. 1930s. 4"h, hand-painted courting scenes in front and back, flowers on side, trimmed with gilt, restoration on handle. $150.00 – 175.00.

Demitasse cup and saucer, c. 1850 – 1900. Round cup, 2⅛" x 1½", gold decoration inside. Saucer, 4⅛", vivid cobalt ground with gilt decoration, courting scene on cup and floral cartouche on saucer. $500.00 – 550.00.

Miniature cup and saucer, c. 1850s. Cup, 1¾" x 1". Saucer, 2⅔". Courting scenes and gilt. $250.00 – 300.00.

Close-up of courting scene.

Platter, c. 1850 – 1924, possible outside painting. 14", hand-painted florals on yellow alternating with courting scenes, gilt. $500.00 – 600.00.

Floral Decoration

"I will be the gladdest thing
under the sun!
I will touch a hundred flowers
And not pick one."

EDNA ST. VINCENT MILLAY
1892 – 1952

Flowers have been among the world's most important decorative motifs. People painted them on their ancient cave walls and glorified them in myths. Flowers have served as inspirations to poets and painters. It was the floral decoration that made the Meissen manufactory famous.

Deutsch Blumen

In the 1730s an independent style of flower painting emerged in Europe, derived from models provided by botanical illustrations in woodcuts and engravings. As a change from the Indianische flowers copied from Japanese Kakiemon and Chinese porcelain, Höroldt developed a new style and technique of flower painting called Deutsch blumen (German flowers) in 1740.

The early Deutsch blumen style was painted with a fine brush in the manner used on ivory miniatures and was of a single or loosely arranged branch placed at random or scattered over the surface of the porcelain. The painting was slow and costly with only six colors in the range. Several had to be fired independently of each other.

The manufactory bought 230 French copperplate flower engravings in 1741. In 1745 they bought the botanic encyclopedia illustrated by the pharmacist Johann Weinmann. These pictures of plants were used as patterns by the painters for their flower and fruit paintings.

At first the German flowers were still and lifeless. The stems were stiff with hanging heads. Some were so realistic they were painted with a shadow and were called ombrierte blumen, or shadowed flowers. They were common garden flowers and insects painted in a very specific manner. They were botanically correct, and even the shadows cast by the flowers were included.

Daisies by C. Klein, postcard.

After 1745 flower painting became livelier. The manufactory began to use mainly German flowers without shadows which were painted from nature. Flowers were grouped together in bouquets or strewn across the surface in sprays. The whole palette of colors was used. Insects and butterflies appeared, adding charm and hiding glaze flaws.

There were hundreds of flowering plants grown at Pellnitz Castle, the summer residence of the Saxon rulers of the eighteenth century, and about six miles from Dresden on the banks of the Elbe River. These plants were organized into nine folio volumes and were financed by Augustus III who was an amateur botanist. He appointed several artists who were graduates of his Dresden Academy of Art as botanical court painters.

During the classical period toward the end of the eighteenth century when Marcolini was director, Meissen flower painting became more functional, symmetrical, and very detailed. This style of flower painting was called Marcolini flower painting.

At the end of the nineteenth century, there was a new and much more flamboyant style of flower painting where painting covered the entire surface of the piece. Around 1920 the Meissen artists used a light, gentle touch on flowers. Wide streaks and soft coloring gave floral bouquets a new look. From this soon developed the Meissen style of floral decoration which continues to be used today.

Carnations by C. Klein, postcard. Meisner & Buch, Leipzig, Kunstier.

The Rose that is sweetest and fairest:
Is the bud that is killed by the frost;
And the love that is dearest and rarest,
Is the true love that we have just lost.

Yellow rose, 1908 postcard.

Strewn Flowers

Since the early nineteenth century, Strewn Flowers has become one of Meissen's best loved patterns. The Strewn Flowers design had a special purpose besides being decorative. A considerable number of early pieces came out of the kilns in perfect shape but with little black spots from iron oxide. These spots could be ground off, but they left a dull spot in the glaze or a pinprick hole. The imperfections could be covered well by painting strewn flowers.

With the emergence of the middle class at the end of the nineteenth century, items with the Strewn Flowers pattern were less expensive than other designs. Today collectors can find some good bargains with this attractive design.

Applied Flowers

The Meissen modelers were also influenced by the painters' interests in flowers. In 1739 Kaendler modeled a vase encrusted with May blossoms or flowers of the Japanese snowball tree. It was so well received that he used applied flowers on open work baskets, covered urns, and vases. He made a coffee service for Maria Josepha in 1739. The entire body of the piece was evenly covered with small individually sculpted flowers.

In 1744 Augustus III needed a royal wedding gift for Count Johann Friedrich and Bernhardina Christina Sophia of Schwarzberg, Rudolstadt. He commissioned a coffee and tea set from Meissen. The set was covered with the delicate May blossom or Snowball decoration. Each snowball blossom was applied by hand. The set is displayed today at the Cincinnati Art Museum.

Applied roses were used frequently as pommels on pot and sugar bowl lids. Diaper patterns of forget-me-nots were used extensively on decorative objects. Each petal

Pair of Meissen vases with applied flowers decoration, displayed in Meissen Exhibition Hall.

and leaf of a flower is shaped one at a time, then joined together to form a realistic flower. It is then hand painted and applied to the object to be decorated.

In the Victorian era massive vases and centerpieces were once again encrusted with May blossoms and were called Schneeballen or Snowball. These ornate pieces command high prices today. They have been widely copied by many smaller German factories throughout the nineteenth and twentieth centuries.

Making of three-dimensional flowers, roses, rosettes, heads, and fruits by a "Bossierer" in Exhibition Hall.

Flower Painters

There were several flower painters that made a considerable impact at the manufactory. A court painter, David Friedrich Weller (1759 – 1789) was one of the outstanding early flower painters during the Marcolini period. He started work at the manufactory in 1781 and just stayed a few years. His style of flower painting was continued by Christian Adolf Heynemann, who was also a court painter. His exceptional work raised the standard of flower painting in the manufactory.

George Friedrich Kersting (1785 – 1847) was head of the painting department in the 1820s. He had a keen sensitivity towards nature and contributed much to flower painting.

Eduard Julius Braunsdorf (1841 – 1922), a well known watercolor and flower painter, was hired by Meissen in 1874. He had a tremendous mastery of the application of color and invented a hazy style. He led flower painting to its highest perfection. He created a technique known as naturalistic flower painting, in which the arrangement of flowers, based on nature, was softly painted in vivid colors.

Otto Eduard Voigt was a flower painter with Braunsdorf. He also worked to develop high temperature paints so that more colors could be used.

Favorite Flowers

Some of the flowers most often used by the Meissen manufactory are the rose, crocus, poppy, morning glory, iris, daisy, carnation, tulip, lily, Chinese aster, primrose, buttercup, honeysuckle, and forget-me-not. A classic Meissen bouquet might have a double rose, blue morning glories, sword lilies, and scattered flowers.

Flowers have been used to express feelings and thoughts, and there are legends and myths surrounding many of them. One of the favorite flowers used by Meissen is the blue forget-me-not. According to legend, a young man and his sweetheart were walking beside the Danube when they came across some blue flowers that grew on an inlet in the middle of the river. The man leapt into the river to pluck them for her. He picked the flower and then got a leg cramp just as he was almost back ashore. As he was caught by the strong currents, he flung the bouquet at her feet with his last strength and cried "Forget-me-not!" and disappeared. She never forgot him and wore the flowers in her hair until her own death.

The iris is the name of the ancient Greek goddess of the rainbow. It represented strength and power to the Egyptians.

The laurel is the symbol of victory and is in Greek and Roman mythology. It stands for triumph and peace. In the nineteenth century Meissen named a cobalt blue underglaze decoration after this plant. With delicate hand painting the small leaves of laurel are applied to the porcelain with a fine brush after the first firing. After the glaze and second burnishing at 1450°C, the Laurel pattern shines in a sparkling blue.

The Mahonia Garland pattern is also in underglaze blue. In a stylistic manner the serrated leaves and berry-like fruits of the Mahonia plant are arranged in a garland. This decoration combines the classical underglaze colors cobalt blue and chrome green.

Professor Heinz Werner created the Orchid on a Branch pattern in 1977 – 1978. It differs from the Blue Onion pattern and is a very stylized orchid design in cobalt blue. The leaves are light green combined with a deep hue of a full green garland of grape leaves.

Early embroidery postcard.

Demitasse cup and saucer, c. 1860 – 1924. Twelve-paneled cup with London-style handle, alternating panels of colorful hand-painted flowers and gilt decoration. $200.00 – 250.00.

Charger, c. 1850 – 1900. 11¾", cobalt blue with white cartouches, hand-painted flowers, gilt. $500.00 – 550.00.

Coffee cup and saucer, c. 1924 – 1934. Flared cup with swan handle, Strewn Flowers with gilt. $150.00 – 175.00.

Teacup, saucer, and plate, c. 1924 – 1934. Scalloped cup and saucer, feathered kicked loop handle, cobalt and gilt rim, lovely hand-painted flowers. $350.00 – 400.00.

Ashtray, c. 1930s. 5", hand-painted orange flowers. $75.00 – 100.00.

Serving bowl or tray, c. 1950s. Scalloped, 10¾", hand-painted sprigs of flowers and gilt rim. $300.00 – 350.00.

Miniature cup and saucer, c. 1840 – 1850. Cup with loop handle, 1⅛"w x 1"h. Deep saucer without well, 2½". Hand-painted Strewn Flowers with gilt. $300.00 – 350.00.

Close-up of decoration.

Candy dish with lid, c. 1850 – 1924, two incised marks. 4½" x 4", hand-painted flowers and gilt. $150.00 – 200.00.

Dresser tray, c. 1950s. Scalloped, 11¼" x 6", hand-painted flowers and heavy gilt. $350.00 – 400.00.

Pair of dessert plates, c. 1930 – 1940s, two incised marks. Plates, 7¼", array of hand-painted flowers in center, heavy gilt on the rim. $125.00 – 150.00 each.

Teacup, saucer, and dessert plate, c. 1950s. Royal Flute cup, 3½"w x 2½". Saucer, 5½", plate 6¾". Colorful hand-painted flowers with gilt. $300.00 – 400.00.

Demitasse cup and saucer, c. 1930s. Cup in Royal Flute shape, 2½"w x 2"h. Saucer, 4". Yellow jonquils and blue forget-me-nots. $200.00 – 225.00.

Show plate, c. 1951 – 1953. Molded gilt rim, 10½", lovely hand-painted flowers in center. $400.00 – 450.00.

Close-up of flower painting.

Demitasse cup and saucer, c. 1930s, two incised marks. Cup, 3"w x 2"h. Saucer, 4⅞". Hand-painted flowers and gilt. $125.00 – 150.00.

Show plate, c. 1930s. 11½", hand-painted flowers and heavy gilt decoration around the floral cartouches. $400.00 – 450.00.

Coffee cup and saucer, c. 1930s. Cup with swan handle, 2½"w x 2"h. Saucer, 5½". Hand-painted flowers and gilt. $200.00 – 250.00.

Close-up of flower painting.

Teacup and saucer, c. 1850 – 1924. Royal Flute shape cup with twisted feather handle, 3¼" x 2¼". Saucer, 5½", Strewn Flowers design. $175.00 – 200.00.

Show plate, c. 1950s. Scalloped, 9¼", array of flowers in center with three cartouches of flowers on border framed by heavy gold, red ground. $400.00 – 450.00.

Close-up of flower painting.

Same plate as above in yellow.

Close-up of flower painting.

Same plate as above in turquoise.

Demitasse set, c. 1920 – 1930. Set includes demitasse pot, teapot, creamer with three paw feet (4" x 4"), sugar (3½" x 3½"), white rose finial with repair, eight demitasse cups with swan handles (2" x 1¾"), and eight saucers (4¼"). Strewn Flowers and gilt. $1,750.00 – 1,800.00.

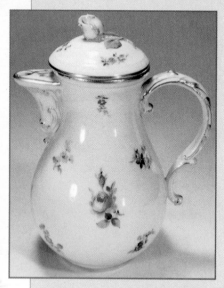

Demitasse pot from above set.

Creamer and sugar.

Close-up of old repair.

Round tray or charger, c. 1924 – 1934. 11¾", hand-painted flowers and heavy gilt. $400.00 – 450.00.

Close-up of gilt decoration

Show plate, c. 1850 – 1924. 8¾", center array of hand-painted flowers with three cartouches with flower sprigs framed in gold, cobalt ground. $350.00 – 400.00.

Serving bowl or tureen, c. 1930s. 10¼" x 6", twisted feather handle on finial, hand-painted flowers and gilt. $500.00 – 600.00.

Close-up of floral painting.

Open salt, c. 1930s. 1⅞" x 1", hand-painted purple flowers and gilt. $80.00 – 95.00.

Open salt with slightly different painting. $80.00 – 95.00.

Miniature cup and saucer, c. 1860 – 1924. Loop handle, deep saucer, hand-painted flowers with gilt. $300.00 – 350.00.

Miniature cup and saucer, c. 1880 – 1920. Rounded cup with loop handle, hand-painted flowers and gilt. $275.00 – 300.00.

Two dessert plates, c. 1850 – 1924, one incised mark. Neumarseille shape, 8¼", hand-painted flowers and gilt. $150.00 – 200.00 each.

Demitasse cup and saucer, c. 1930s. Cup in Royal Flute shape; hand-painted orange flowers, no gilt. $125.00 – 150.00.

Demitasse cup and saucer, c. 1953 – 1957, two incised marks. Cup in Royal Flute shape, 2½" x 2". Saucer, 4¼". Hand-painted flowers with gilt. $100.00 – 125.00.

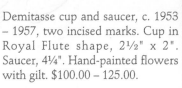

Teapot, c. 1850 – 1924. Branch spout and handle, 6½" x 7½", yellow rose finial on lid, hand-painted Strewn Flowers and gilt. $300.00 – 350.00.

Close-up of green roses.

Demitasse cup and saucer, c. 1930s. Cup in Royal Flute shape with embossed mold, 2½" x 2". Saucer, 4⅓". Hand-painted green roses and gilt. $225.00 – 250.00.

Close-up of swan handle.

Coffee cup and saucer, c. 1824 – 1850.
Cup with swan handle, 2⅓" x 2".
Saucer, 5½", hand-painted flowers
and gilt. $200.00 – 250.00.

Close-up of flower painting.

Fruit bowl, c. 1870. Reticulated border,
10" x 6¼", full flower and insect painting.
$500.00 – 550.00.

Coffee cup and saucer, c. 1850 –
1924, one incised mark. Cup with
swan handle, hand-painted Strewn
Flowers and gilt. $100.00 – 125.00.

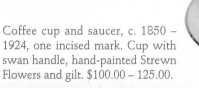

Demitasse cup and saucer, c. 1950 – 1960s. Footed and flared cup, 2⅞" x 2". Saucer, 4⅞". Eight-petal cobalt design with hand-painted flowers and gilt. $175.00 – 200.00.

Coffeepot, c. 1850 – 1924. Snake handle and dragon spout, 10", hand-painted flowers and gilt. $500.00 – 550.00.

Demitasse cup and saucer, c. 1850 – 1924. Cup with twig handle with flower and leaf extensions, 2⅓" x 2". Saucer, 4⅔". Strewn Flowers and gilt. $175.00 – 200.00.

Close-up of finial.

Teapot, c. 1850 – 1924. 6½" x 7½", rosebud finial on lid, vivid full flower painting. $350.00 – 400.00.

Teacup and saucer, c. 1930s. Scalloped cup with kicked loop handle, 3¾" x 2". Saucer, 5¾". Strewn Flowers, no gilt. $125.00 – 150.00.

Teacup and saucer,
1900 – 1924. Hand-
painted yellow
flowers and gilt.
$150.00 – 200.00.

Plate, c. 1850 – 1924.
Scalloped, 9¼", cobalt
border with three floral
cartouches, exceptional
full flower painting in
center. $400.00 – 500.00.

Demitasse cup and saucer, c. 1930s,
two incised marks. Cup in Royal
Flute shape, hand-painted flowers,
gilt line on rims. $100.00 – 125.00.

Miniature pitcher, c. 1850 –
1900. 2½", three twig feet,
branch handle, cobalt ground
with gilt decoration and floral
cartouches. $175.00 – 200.00.

Demitasse cup and saucer, c. 1900 – 1924.
Quatrefoil shaped cup with Dresden handle,
2⅔" x 3" x 1½". Saucer, 4¼" x 4⅔". Strewn
Flowers and gilt. $150.00 – 200.00.

Close-up of painting.

Another view of bowl.

Bowl, c. 1850 – 1924. Scalloped, 4½" x 3¾", applied forget-me-nots on outside, hand-painted flowers inside. $250.00 – 300.00.

Bottom of bowl showing applied forget-me-nots.

Charger or show plate, c. 1850 – 1900. 11¼", cobalt blue with array of hand-painted flowers in center and floral cartouches framed with gilt. $400.00 – 500.00.

Close-up of floral painting.

Set of 12 dessert plates, c. 1880s. 8", decorated with Full Flower painting with a gold band on border. $1,500.00 – 1,800.00.

One plate of set.

Coffee cup and saucer, c. 1850 – 1900. Cup with 1" gold band inside, high swan handle, 3" x 3". Saucer, 5½". Hand-painted flowers. $175.00 – 200.00.

Close-up of flower painting.

Dish, c. 1850 – 1924. Quatrefoil, 6" x 4½", Full Flower painting with gilt border. $140.00 – 160.00.

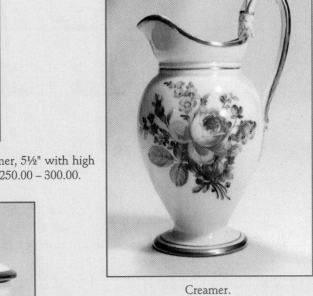

Sugar and creamer, c. 1850 – 1924. Sugar, 4". Creamer, 5½" with high feathered handle. Full Flower decoration with gilt. $250.00 – 300.00.

Creamer.

Sugar.

Chocolate pot, c. 1824 – 1850. Ornate swan handle, 8½". Full Flower painting and lavish gilt. $400.00 – 500.00.

Back view.

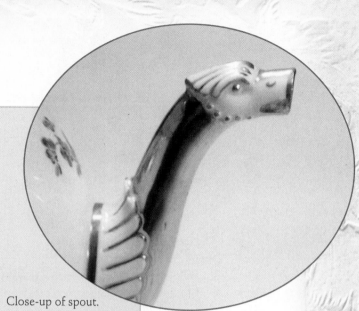

Close-up of spout.

Teapot, c. 1820s. Serpent spout and ornate feathered handle, 8¼" x 7". Full Flower painting with lavish gilt. $400.00 – 500.00.

Close-up of floral painting.

Close-up of floral painting.

Coffeepot, c. 1840s. Serpent spout and ornate feathered handle, 9", beautiful Full Flower painting and gilt. $450.00 – 550.00.

Coffee cup and saucer, c. 1850 – 1900. Cup with swan handle, 2¾" x 2½". Saucer, 5½". Full Flowers and gilt. $250.00 – 350.00.

Close-up of saucer.

Another cup and saucer with different flowers.

Another cup and saucer with different flowers.

Demitasse cup and saucer, c. 1850 – 1924. Cup with high swan handle, 2¼" x 2". Saucer, 4½". Full Flower painting with a butterfly and gilt. $275.00 – 375.00.

Teapot, c. 1850 – 1900.
Melon-shaped, 6"h, twisted
feather handle, Full Flower
painting. $450.00 – 550.00.

Back view.

Close-up of flower finial.

Close-up of flower painting.

Teacup and saucer, c. 1774 – 1814. Cup
with square handle, 2⅞" x 1¾". Saucer,
5¼". Full Flower painting. $400.00 – 450.00.

Coffeepot, c. 1850 – 1924. Feathered spout and handle, rose finial on lid, 9"h, blue flowers and insects with gilt trim. $400.00 – 450.00.

Close-up of finial.

Close-up of flower painting.

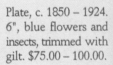

Plate, c. 1850 – 1924. 6", blue flowers and insects, trimmed with gilt. $75.00 – 100.00.

Cream pitcher, c. 1850 – 1924. Three curved feet, 3½", blue flowers and gilt, chip on top of one foot. $75.00 – 100.00.

Another view of tureen.

Tureen, c. 1850 – 1900. Ornate mold with curled feet
and two aqua feathered handles, cupid finial with
a cornucopia with fruit spilling out, 13" x 9¾",
hand-painted flowers and bugs.
$1,000.00 – 1,200.00.

Close-up of the cupid.

Demitasse cup and saucer, c. 1924 – 1934. Cup,
2⅓" x 1⅞". Saucer, 4⅛". Hand-painted flowers with gilt on rims. $200.00 – 250.00.

Demitasse cup and saucer, c. 1924 – 1934. Cup, 2⅓" x 1⅞".
Saucer, 4⅛". Hand-painted flowers with gilt on rims.
$200.00 – 250.00.

Demitasse cup and saucer, c. 1924 – 1934. Cup, 2⅓" x 1⅞". Saucer, 4⅛". Hand-painted flowers with gilt on rims. $200.00 – 250.00.

Demitasse cup and saucer, c. 1924 – 1934. Cup, 2⅓" x 1⅞". Saucer, 4⅛". Hand-painted flowers with gilt on rims. $200.00 – 250.00.

Demitasse cup and saucer, c. 1850 – 1924. Cup in Royal Flute pattern, 2⅓" x 1⅞". Saucer, 4⅛". Hand-painted flowers and gilt. $225.00 – 275.00.

Demitasse cup and saucer, c. 1930s. Scalloped cup with six feet, twisted branch handle, applied flowers. $600.00 – 700.00.

Miniature cup and saucer, c. 1850 – 1900. Can-shaped cup, 1⅛" x 1"h. Saucer, 2½". Hand-painted flowers and gilt. $300.00 – 350.00.

Demitasse pot, c. 1924 – 1934. Feathered spout, 7½" x 6¼". Yellow rose finial, hand-painted flowers and gilt. $400.00 – 500.00.

Demitasse cup and saucer, c. 1850 – 1924. Cup in Royal Flute pattern, 2⅓" x 1⅞". Saucer, 4⅛". Hand-painted flowers and gilt. $225.00 – 275.00.

Coffee cup, saucer and dessert plate, c. 1924 – 1934. Cup in Royal Flute shape, 3½"w x 2½"h. Saucer, 5½". Plate, 6¾". Hand-painted flowers and gilt. $300.00 – 375.00.

Coffee cup, saucer, and dessert plate, c. 1924 – 1934. Cup in Royal Flute shape, 3½"w x 2½"h. Saucer, 5½". Plate, 6¾". Hand-painted flowers and gilt. $300.00 – 375.00.

Close-up of floral cartouche.

Coffee cup and saucer, c. 1850 – 1900. Cup in can shape, floral cartouche, cobalt with gilt decoration. $600.00 – 650.00.

Coffee cup and saucer, c. 1850 – 1924. Cup in
Royal Flute shape, Strewn Flowers with gilt.
$150.00 – 175.00.

Plate, c. 1850 – 1924. 8¼", rich cobalt blue with
three floral cartouches, gilt.
$600.00 – 700.00.

Demitasse cup and saucer, c. 1850 – 1924. Quatrefoil shaped cup
with Dresden handle, Strewn Flowers with decorative gilt
pattern on rims. $200.00 – 250.00.

Coffee cup and saucer, c. 1924 – 1934. Straight-
sided cup with loop handle and inner spur,
hand-painted flowers and gilt.
$150.00 – 200.00.

Demitasse cup and saucer, c. 1900.
Cup with swan handle, 2" x 1¾".
Saucer, 4¼". Strewn Flowers and
gilt. $150.00 – 175.00.

Plate, c. 1924 – 1934. 6¼", hand-painted
flowers and gilt. $100.00 – 150.00.

Coffee cup and saucer, c. 1850 – 1900. Cup in Royal Flute
shape, 2¾" x 2½". Saucer, 5¼". Hand-painted blue
flowers and insects, gilt. $125.00 – 175.00.

Plate, c. 1924 – 1934. 6¼", hand-painted
flowers and gilt. $100.00 – 150.00.

Demitasse cup and saucer, c. 1850 – 1900. Cup, 2⅞" x 2".
Saucer, 4⅞". Heavy gold, hand-painted flowers.
$275.00 – 300.00.

Close-up of Iris.

Demitasse cup and
saucer, c. 1950s. Scal-
loped cup, 2¾" x 1½".
Saucer, 4¾". Hand-
painted purple Iris and
gilt. $175.00 – 200.00.

Demitasse cup and saucer, c. 1850 – 1924. Cup with six feet, twisted branch handle, applied and hand-painted flowers. $550.00 – 600.00.

Plate, c. 1850 – 1924. 9¾", exceptional hand-painted flowers on unusual chocolate brown ground. $1,500.00 – 1,600.00.

Close-up of flower painting.

Coffee cup and saucer, c. 1890 – 1924. Cup with Swan handle, gold border inside cup and on saucer rim, blue flowers. $200.00 – 250.00.

Teacup and saucer, c. 1774 – 1814. Cup with twisted feather handle, 3" x 1⅞". Saucer, 5¼", hand-painted flowers with gilt on rim. $350.00 – 450.00.

Of all the flowers, roses have been used the most by poets and artists as symbols of love and to show the fragility and brevity of life. There is a tremendous variety of roses in existence, and many have made their appearance in European art.

The world's oldest living rose is thought to be 1,000 years old. It continues to grow on the walls of the Hildesheim Cathedral in Germany. Recently, archeologists have discovered the fossilized remains of wild roses over 400 million years old.

Legends

There are many legends about the rose. According to Greek mythology, Aphrodite gave the rose its name. She was said to have sprung from the foam of the sea. The white foam clinging to her arms and legs turned into sweet roses. Thus, the rose is her symbol, the symbol of love.

It is said that the floors of Cleopatra's palace were carpeted with delicate rose petals. Confucius had a 600 book library on how to care for roses. Shakespeare refers to roses more than 50 times throughout his writing, such as: "Wherefore are thou rose...?"

Many Meissen dinnerware sets were made with the Rose pattern between the 1890s and 1930s. Numerous sets were exported to the United States and England. Some were plain, and other sets were enhanced with gold trim. A vari-

Rose, 1909 German postcard.

ety of accessory serving pieces were produced, such as tureens, platters, vases, gravy boats, ladles, trivets, and ashtrays. It is possible for collectors to put together a complete Rose pattern dinnerware service today quite reasonably priced.

Many pieces of the Meissen Rose pattern found in the marketplace today have two incised marks through the crossed swords, which usually mean second quality. There are several probable reasons for this. First, because the items with the Rose pattern were moderately priced, the Meissen manufactory may have allocated second quality white ware for this pattern. Secondly, since the Rose pattern is a fairly simple, repetitive design, it may have been painted by student artists or those with little experience. A third explanation might be that because the demand for this pattern was so great, Meissen may have contracted with outside decorators to paint the design.

2003 Rose Exhibition

Rose, postcard, Meissner & Buch-Leipzig-Kuntsier.

On October 18, 2003, Meissen held a special exhibition at the manufactory to honor the history of the Rose decoration. Over 250 porcelain pieces displaying the rose included a splendid cup in the form of a rose exemplifying the Rococo age, a dejeuner with the classic Rose pattern, and the new Prickly Rose decoration on the new Wave design created by Gudrun Gaube. A new white rose with a purple center was created by Meissen's artists specially for this exhibition as well as a limited edition golden rose signet.

Set of 12 dessert bowls, c. 1937, two incised marks. Slightly scalloped, measuring 5½" each, hand-painted roses, no gilt. $300.00 – 350.00.

Cake plate, c. 1850 – 1924. Two-handled, 11½", molded design by handles, hand-painted rose in center, buds on border, no gilt. $150.00 – 175.00.

Demitasse pot, c. 1924 – 1934. 6¼" h, chips on applied rose finial on lid, well-painted rose. $350.00 – 400.00.

Close-up of rose finial.

Covered casserole, c. 1924 – 1934, two incised marks. Footed with ornate leafy handles, unusual finial, hand-painted roses with gilt. $400.00 – 450.00.

Set of 12 soup bowls, c. 1930s, two incised marks. Scalloped, 8½" each, rose painting, no gilt. $350.00 – 400.00.

Turkey platter, c. 1930s. Two handles, 20" x 14", rose painting with gilt. $600.00 – 700.00.

Another view.

Serving bowl, c. 1900 – 1924. 9"w x 3"h, rose painting with gilt. $350.00 – 400.00.

Serving bowl, c. 1930s, four incised marks. 10½" x 3¾", hand-painted roses and gilt. $300.00 – 350.00.

Soup plate, c. 1930s. Scalloped, deep, 9", roses with gilt.
$75.00 – 100.00.

Serving platter, c. 1930s, two incised marks.
Round, scalloped, 11", roses and gilt.
$350.00 – 400.00.

Vase, c. 1929. Flared, 5¼"h, gold band inside rim, hand-painted flowers, gilt trim. $175.00 – 200.00.

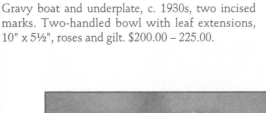

Gravy boat and underplate, c. 1930s, two incised marks. Two-handled bowl with leaf extensions, 10" x 5½", roses and gilt. $200.00 – 225.00.

Gravy boat, underplate and ladle, c. 1900 – 1924. Two-handled bowl, 10" x 5½". Ladle with twisted stem handle, hand-painted roses with gilt. $350.00 – 400.00.

Open salt and pepper, c. 1930s. Two bowls with handle, 3¾" x 1¼", hand-painted rose on one side, bud on other, gilt. $125.00 – 150.00.

Trivet, c. 1930s, two incised marks. Round with four ball feet, 6", hand-painted roses and gilt. $125.00 – 150.00.

Coffee set, c. 1850 – 1924. Set includes pot (10"h), covered sugar (4½" x 4¼"), and creamer (5"h). Minor chips on rose finials, roses and gilt. $650.00 – 700.00.

Coffeepot.

Tea set, c. 1900 – 1924. Set includes teapot (9½" x 5½"), sugar (4" x 4"), and creamer (5"). Minor chips on finial roses, roses and gilt trim on rims, spout, and handles. $650.00 – 700.00.

Teapot from preceding set.

Ashtray, c. 1930s, two incised marks.
5", hand-painted roses and gilt.
$60.00 – 75.00.

Teacup and saucer, c. 1930s,
two incised marks. Royal
Flute cup with deep saucer,
rose painting.
$90.00 – 115.00.

Demitasse cup and saucer, c. 1924 – 1934. Cup
with swan handle, hand-painted roses and gilt.
$150.00 – 175.00.

Close-up of rose painting.

Coffee set, c. 1850 – 1924. Set includes coffeepot with high swan handle (7" x 9½"), creamer (3¼" x 5½"), and sugar bowl (3½" x 3½"). Rose painting, heavy gilt trim. $600.00 – 700.00.

Coffee cup and saucer, c. 1930s, two incised marks. Royal Flute cup with deep saucer, rose painting. $90.00 – 115.00.

Charger, c. 1950s, two incised marks. Scalloped, with molded daisies and gilt leaves, 11¾", large hand-painted rose in center. $300.00 – 350.00.

Close-up of cup.

Demitasse cup and saucer, c. 1850 – 1924. Cup, 2⅔"w x 2¼", with snake handle. Saucer, 4½". Garland of small roses and gilt with torch and scepter on cup. $200.00 – 250.00.

Single plate from set at left.

Set of 12 dessert plates, c. 1924 – 1934, two incised marks. 7" each, rose painting with gilt. $500.00 – 550.00.

Vase, c. 1930s. Flared, 5¼" x 6½", hand-painted roses and gilt. $275.00 – 300.00.

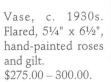

Close-up of rose finial.

Coffee set, c. 1924 – 1934. Set includes coffeepot (7½" x 10½"), sugar (4"), and creamer (5¼"). Applied roses on finials on lids, hand-painted roses with gilt. $600.00 – 650.00.

Serving tray, c. 1924 – 1934, two incised marks. 13", roses and gilt. $300.00 – 350.00.

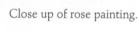

Close up of rose painting.

Pitcher, c. 1924 – 1934. 5¼" x 5", roses and gilt. $100.00 – 125.00.

Trivet, c. 1924 – 1934. Four ball feet, 5¾", rose and gilt. $175.00 – 200.00.

Another view.

Platter, c. 1930s.
Scalloped, 11",
roses and gilt.
$400.00 – 450.00.

Demitasse cup and saucer, c. 1824 – 1850.
Cup with loop handle and rose painting,
buds on saucer. $125.00 – 150.00.

Set of 11 dinner
plates, c. 1930s,
two incised marks.
Scalloped, 9½"
each, rose painting.
$500.00 – 600.00.

One plate
from
above set.

Teacup and saucer, c. 1924 – 1934, two
incised marks. Cup in Royal Flute shape,
twisted feather handle, hand-painted
roses and gilt. $100.00 – 125.00.

Set of 11 bread and butter plates, c. 1900 – 1924. Scalloped, 6¼"each, rose painting. $400.00 – 500.00.

Covered water pitcher, c. 1850 – 1924. Bulbous, bud finial on lid, 7½", hand-painted roses. $200.00 – 250.00.

Single plate from above set.

Serving dish, c. 1930s. Square, scalloped, 7¼", roses and gilt. $250.00 – 275.00.

Set of 10 dessert plates, c. 1850 – 1924. Scalloped, 7"each, rose painting with gilt. $300.00 – 350.00.

Vegetable bowl, c. 1930s, two incised marks. Scalloped, 10" x 6¾", rose painting and gilt, some wear on gilt. $150.00 – 200.00.

Photograph of mark.

Set of seven salad plates, c. 1930s, mark partially removed. Scalloped, with gilt. $350.00 – 400.00.

Set of six dinner plates, c. 1850 – 1924. Scalloped, 9¾", roses and gold. $600.00 – 700.00.

Coffeepot, c. 1930s. Curled broken loop handle, rose finial on lid, 10", roses and gilt. $300.00 – 350.00.

Serving bowl, c. 1930s. Oval, 11¼" x 7¾",
roses and gold. $350.00 – 400.00.

Tray or platter, c. 1924 – 1934. Round,
scalloped, 11", roses and gilt.
$400.00 – 450.00.

Demitasse cup and saucer, c. 1930s, two incised marks. Cup
in Royal Flute form, 2" x 2". Saucer, 4½". Roses,
no gold trim. $90.00 – 115.00.

Saucer, c. 1900 – 1924. Scalloped,
5¼", roses and gilt.
$35.00 – 40.00.

Bouillon cup and saucer, c.
1930s. Royal Flute cup with
two handles, hand-painted
roses. $100.00 – 125.00.

History

Long before Meissen became a city of porcelain, it was a city of wine. For 800 years the vicinity along the Elbe riverbanks has been a wine-growing region. It is not surprising that the cultivation of wine has influenced Meissen's designs.

From the beginning of the Meissen manufactory, vine leaves and grapes were sculpted in relief on even the earliest unpainted vessels. During the Baroque and Rococo periods, both individual porcelain figures and groups were created around the subject of wine.

During the time of Neoclassicism, 1775 – 1820, classical Greek and Roman design elements strongly influenced the shapes and designs of Meissen porcelain. It was defined by simple, quite functional classical forms. A good example of classicism is the Full Green Vine Wreath or the Vine Leaf Garland pattern. It was developed in 1817 by Meissen flower painter Johann Samuel Arnhold (1766 – 1828) shortly after a new green underglaze paint made from chromium-oxide was developed by

Art Nouveau lady with grapes, French postcard, 997 E. Deully.

workers at the manufactory. This green paint could withstand the 1450°C firing and, therefore, could be painted before the porcelain was glazed. The dinnerware shape for this pattern was created in 1820 by Johann Daniel Schöne (1767 – 1843) and has been a standard part of Meissen's inventory ever since.

Technique

Meissen's technique for the popular Vine Leaf Garland pattern has remained almost the same since it was developed in 1817. The blackish-green leaves are painted by using the underglaze technique. The leaves are copied with a stencil. The same shapes always appear at regular intervals on a painted piece. With the stencils, only the outline of the green leaves are cut out. The black stems and leaf ribs are added freehand.

The Meissen chromium green is unusually deep and yet strongly radiates warmth. Because it is painted under the glaze, it takes on a softness that cannot be attained over the glaze. The deepness of the green is so strong that at a distance, you can no longer see the black ribs of the leaves.

A water soluble paint is used, which is brushed on quite thick. In its catalog, *Vine Leaf Garland*, Meissen says, "It is sucked up quite hungrily by the raw, unglazed porcelain." Each grape leaf is given its three central veins, which are then amplified with fine, straight branches. Then the leaves are attached.

Vine Leaf Today

The Vine Leaf Garland pattern, or Vine Leaf for short, remains a top seller for Meissen today. The modern version has a much looser arrangement of grape leaves. As a result it goes better with the modern porcelain shapes, such as the Waves design. It shows grapes in the background which are painted very softly with a gentle touch in a pale green color. The contours of the leaves are kept flowing around, and the veins flow in a smooth s-curve.

The deep green tones are the same, but the grapes are painted in the lightest green and shimmer giving off a light gray cast. Meissen has also created a new rich pattern with overglaze gold veins and a gold border.

Today the Vine Leaf pattern is very popular. It is also practical — its underglaze painting is dishwasher-proof. The combination of white and dark green is most attractive and is frequently used during the Christmas holidays.

Coffee cup and saucer, c. 1930s. Cup with swan handle, 3¼"w x 2¾". Saucer, 6"w, Vine Leaf Garland pattern with gilt. $125.00 – 150.00.

Teacup and saucer, c. 1930s, two incised marks. Scalloped cup with kicked loop handle, 3¾" x 2". Saucer, 6", Vine Leaf Garland pattern. $75.00 – 100.00.

Tea set, c. 1930s. Set includes teapot, covered sugar, and creamer. Vine Leaf Garland pattern. $400.00 – 500.00.

Another view.

Coffee cup and saucer, c. 1930s. Flared cup with swan handle, 3¼" x 2¾". Saucer, 6". Vine Leaf Garland pattern, no gilt. $100.00 – 125.00.

Demitasse cup and saucer, c. 1850 – 1924. Cup in Royal Flute shape, 2½" x 1¾". Saucer, 4¼". Vine Leaf Garland pattern with gilt. $150.00 – 175.00.

Pot de crème, c. 1950s. Cup with loop handle, flower bud finial on lid, Vine Leaf Garland pattern. $125.00 – 150.00.

Coffee cup and saucer, c. 1850 – 1924. Flared cup with swan handle, 3¼" x 2¾". Vine Leaf Garland pattern with heavy gilt. $175.00 – 200.00.

Demand for Oriental Porcelain

The Dutch ships of the East India Company had begun regular sailings to China in the 1600s. Spices, fabrics, and the exotic drink of tea were introduced to Europe. Much of the appeal of tea drinking was the result of the delicate blue and white porcelain teapots and tea bowls that were brought over from China. Owning this lovely porcelain became a status symbol throughout Europe.

After the collapse of the Ming Dynasty in 1644, the East Indian merchants turned to Japan. Their brightly enameled wares were immediately sought after, and for the first time colored wares reached the west. Kakiemon ware originated between 1670 and 1690 and depicted flowers, insects, and birds.

Chinese and Japanese porcelain met a demand in Europe. Three new hot drinks were the rage — tea, coffee, and chocolate, and there was a need for utensils to serve and to drink these beverages. Both princes and wealthy aristocrats surrounded themselves with the products of East Asia. Fabrics, furniture, and porcelain were avidly collected. There was a fascination with the East and anything associated with it. Anything Oriental was linked to the East India Company and was described as "Indian."

In 1720 Höroldt was ordered by Augustus the Strong to copy as many Oriental pieces as possible. Höroldt studied copper engravings with chinoiseries (Chinese type motifs), as well as actual examples of Chinese and Japanese porcelain from the royal collection in Dresden. He drew several hundred paintings of small Chinese and Japanese scenes which served as patterns for Meissen's new Indian decoration.

Today Meissen's Japanese and Chinese motifs are still called Indian painting. At the present, Meissen carries more than 250 kinds of Indian paintings.

Bowl with Chinese decoration. Postcard published by National Palace Museum, Taipei, Republic of China.

Popular Indian Patterns

Indian Flowers

The term Indianische blumen (East Indies flowers) refers to a style of floral decoration introduced by Höroldt in 1720. It was influenced by the Japanese Kakiemon style and Chinese famille verte (green palette wares).

The Indian flower decorations of the Meissen manufactory were mostly derived from the plant subjects of Chinese and Japanese porcelain painters. Typical flowers used were: pine, bamboo, prunus, peony, chrysanthemum, camellia, wild rose, cherry blossom, pomegranate blossom, iris, and the magnolia. A few Chinese plants were imported into Europe, and considerable interest was generated in the botanical world.

One of the richest Indian patterns developed by Meissen in the 1740s is referred to as Indian Painting with Gold Dots. It is a stylized flower spray that resembles a peony. At first it was painted in a very free and loose style. Now the pattern is stabilized on every piece by the use of a stencil. The result is a very disciplined painting. It can be found in a variety of colors, including purple, green, blue and black. In the book, *Painting Porcelain in the Meissen Style*, Uwe Geissler says, "This extremely decorative painting has enjoyed lasting popularity for centuries among porcelain fans."

Two Meissen bottle vases with Indian flowers. Postcard from Meissen Museum, courtesy of Meissen.

Chinese Festival dragon from Hong Kong. Postcard © Commonwealth Institute, Kensington High Street, London, W.8.6NQ.

Dragon Patterns

The dragon was revered in China as a symbol of happiness and fertility as early as the seventh century. It was also on the coat-of-arms of the Chinese Emperor. Dragons with five claws were reserved for the Imperial Emperor only. Dragons with four claws were allowed for Imperial princes, and those with three claws were for officials of the Imperial court.

COURT DRAGON PATTERN

The Court Dragon is the earliest and most well known Indian decoration on Meissen porcelain. It was used for one of the first dinner services for the Dresden court in 1730. Two long red dragons and two groups of symbols are on the border of the item. In the center there are two phoenix birds arranged in a circle.

In China the dragon's counterpart is the bird which is called phoenix in English. In Japan it is named hoo and in China it is called feng-huang. It is on the coat-of-arms of the Chinese Empress and symbolizes summer. The original Court Dragon pattern was always painted in red as this color was thought to be a safeguard against demons and other dangers in China.

All Meissen ware decorated with the red Court Dragon pattern was strictly reserved for the electoral court until 1918. From the middle of the nineteenth century on, the pattern was produced for sale to the public in colors other than red. The Court Dragon pattern is still popular today, and it can be found on all dinnerware items in black, brown, yellow, red, blue, green, and purple.

Phoenix type birds, early Swiss postcard.

MING DRAGON PATTERN

Another popular dragon pattern made by Meissen is the Ming Dragon. In China, porcelain portraying Ming dragons was reserved for Imperial Princes. Sometimes single dragons, as well as pairs, are shown with flaming pearls. If the dragon is swallowing the pearl, it represents the waning moon. If the dragon spews forth the pearl, it represents a growing moon. Today Meissen makes the Ming Dragon pattern in eight color schemes.

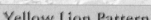

Yellow Lion Pattern

Dinnerware from Yellow Lion pattern, Meissen Museum.

According to Chinese legend, the tiger is the king of all four-legged animals. It symbolizes autumn. In Japanese legend, the tiger represents courage and strength. In Japanese porcelain decorations, the combination of tiger and prunus blossoms symbolizes strength, determination, and longevity. A yellow tiger signifies fame, while a red one is life-giving.

The tiger was used on Meissen items as early as 1728. An early dinner service made for the king was known as the Yellow Lion service. It was actually a tiger with bamboo and a plum tree. In the 1733 inventory of the Dresden Court household, it was renamed Golden Lion. It was made well into the twentieth century, and pieces having this decoration are eagerly sought by collectors.

Kakiemon Decoration

Kakiemon is a style of Japanese porcelain that was created in Arita by the Japanese ceramicist Salaida Kizaemon, known as Kakiemon I (1569 – 1666). He was the first to produce porcelain with overglaze polychrome enamels. His family continued to produce this type of ware for several centuries.

Kakiemon wares are characterized by simple naturalistic designs covering about two-thirds of an object. The palette includes red, blue, yellow, black, purple, and green enamels. Occasionally gilt was added to the design.

Augustus the Strong had a large collection of Japanese Kakiemon porcelain displayed in the Japanese Palace. Many of these pieces were made available to the factory to copy in the 1720s. The Kakiemon originals included square sake bottles, octagonal bowls, flower petal-shaped dishes, and hexagonal vases with covers. All these shapes were copied at Meissen.

A style of porcelain decoration soon developed at Meissen which, though Japanese in style, became more European in influence. Meissen painters arranged their principal subject in the center of an object and filled the empty spaces with strewn flowers. The Meissen pieces were more rigid in form than the Japanese originals, and the decoration was usually more brilliant and precise.

In the 1730s a set of Meissen plates was decorated in the Kakiemon style. The plates were 12-sided with two herons, one standing and one flying, and a peony branch painted in enamel colors and gilt. The heron was the symbol of long life and a favorite subject of the Japanese. These plates are displayed in the Zwinger Museum in Dresden.

There are many Kakiemon patterns adapted by the Meissen manufactory. The Flying Squirrel is a Kakiemon pattern that has brushwood fences, flowers, bamboo, and a flying red squirrel. It has also been described as a flying fox or dog.

In Meissen Indian paintings, the crane has been combined with various parts of flowers and plants or shown standing amid a rocky landscape. The crane is the symbol of longevity and is deeply revered by the Japanese.

A number of Japanese branch paintings were adapted by Meissen. These often include the bamboo, the prunus (winter plum blossom), and the pine, which were favorite figural subjects in Japan. The bamboo is the symbol of man, and the prunus is the symbol of strength. The pine is green all year long and represents true and lasting friendship. These three plants together symbolize desirability, longevity, and vitality since all keep their leaves and blossoms in the winter.

Painting of Indian Decoration

Many generations of Meissen painters have contributed to the variety of Indian painting motifs. The Meissen painter has a selection of 160 colors. Copper colors are frequently used. Aside from their brilliance, they are transparent, somewhat like glass. Thus, a drawing that has been covered with copper paints will become visible after firing.

After the paint has been brought to the correct consistency, the painter draws the outline of the decoration onto the porcelain with a steel pen. Once the paint has dried well, areas of emphasis can be applied. These provide accents in the decoration and determine the color shade.

Master painters in the art of Indian painting are entrusted with the most difficult work of all — the decoration of "royal vases." The prototype of these vases was made at the beginning of the eighteenth century for the court of Augustus after old East Asia originals. The outline is drawn on the vases and lids with a brush, not

Meissen Indian decoration, Meissen demonstration studio, Exhibition Hall.

with a steel pen. These vases are put in special fixtures which hold them in a firm position and provide a board on which the artist may rest his arm.

Teapot with strainer, c. 1850 – 1924. 9" x 6", rose finial on lid, Purple Indian pattern, gilt. $600.00 – 700.00.

Close-up of lid with rose finial.

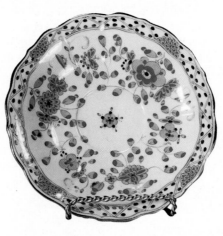

Teacup and saucer, c. 1860 – 1924. Twelve-lobed cup with kicked loop handle with thumb rest, Purple Indian pattern. $250.00 – 350.00.

Set of 10 plates, c. 1880 – 1900. 8¼"each, Purple Indian pattern. $1,000.00 – 1,100.00.

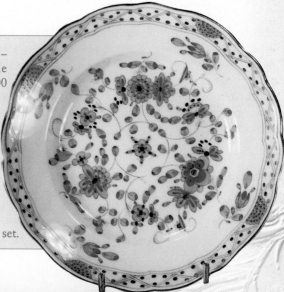

Single plate from set.

Coffee cup and saucer, c. 1860 – 1924. Oval quatrefoil cup with pinched loop handle, Purple Indian pattern. $250.00 – 350.00.

Demitasse cup and saucer, c. 1860 – 1924. Quatrefoil cup with wishbone handle, Purple Indian pattern. $250.00 – 350.00.

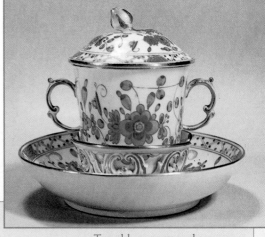

Demitasse cup and saucer, c. 1850 – 1920. Quatrefoil shaped cup, 2½". Saucer, 4½" x 5¼". Purple Indian pattern. $250.00 – 275.00.

Another view of trembleuse.

Trembleuse cup and saucer, c. 1850 – 1924. Cup with two broken loop handles, saucer with reticulated rail, rose finial on lid, Purple Indian pattern. $500.00 – 600.00.

Close-up of lid.

Creamer and covered sugar, c. 1850 – 1900. Creamer with branch handle, 4" x 3¼". Applied rose finial on lid of sugar, 4¾" x 3¾". Purple Indian pattern. $300.00 – 350.00.

Coffeepot, c. 1850 – 1924. 10", lid with rose finial, Purple Indian pattern, gilt. $400.00 – 450.00.

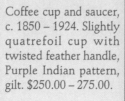

Close-up of pattern.

Coffee cup and saucer, c. 1850 – 1924. Slightly quatrefoil cup with twisted feather handle, Purple Indian pattern, gilt. $250.00 – 275.00.

Close-up of bobeches.

Pair of candleholders with detachable bobeches, c. 1850 – 1924. 9", eight leafy points on bobeches, Purple Indian pattern, some chips. $400.00 – 450.00.

Serving bowl, c. 1850 – 1924. Scalloped, 9¼", Purple Indian pattern, gilt. $250.00 – 300.00.

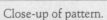

Close-up of pattern.

Coffee cup and saucer, c. 1850 – 1900. Scalloped cup with twisted leaf handle, Purple Indian pattern, no gilt trim. $250.00 – 300.00.

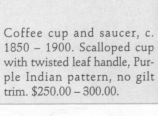

Creamer and sugar, c. 1850 – 1924. Creamer with three branch feet, quatrefoil sugar, rose finial on lid, Purple Indian pattern, gilt. $300.00 – 350.00.

Creamer from above set.

Trembleuse, c. 1930s. Two-handled cup, 2⅞" x 3", applied rose on lid. Saucer with attached rail, 5⅔". Purple Indian pattern. $500.00 – 575.00.

Another view.

Shoe, c. 1900. 6½", Purple Indian pattern. $300.00 – 375.00.

Teacup and saucer, c. 1774 – 1814. Cup with twisted feather handle, 3⅛" x 2". Saucer, 5¼". Purple Indian flowers. $300.00 – 350.00.

Demitasse cup and saucer, c. 1850 – 1900. Cup in Royal Flute shape, 2½" x 1¾". Saucer, 4¼". Purple Indian pattern. $200.00 – 250.00.

Teacup and saucer, c. 1774 – 1814. Cup with twisted handle, 3" x 2". Saucer, 5". Oriental flowers with band of puce decoration. $300.00 – 350.00.

Coffee cup and saucer, c. 1850 – 1924. Cup in Royal Flute shape, hand-painted Court Dragon pattern in purple. $250.00 – 300.00.

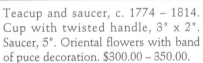

Close-up of decoration.

Coffee cup and saucer, c. 1850 – 1924. Cup in Royal Flute shape, hand-painted Court Dragon pattern in green. $250.00 – 300.00.

Dish in green Court Dragon pattern.

Set of eight mint dishes, c. 1950s. Scalloped, 3¼"w x 1¾"h, Court Dragon pattern in different colors. $300.00 – 350.00.

Dish in yellow Court Dragon pattern.

Dish in black Court Dragon pattern.

Close-up of birds in center.

Dish in pink Court Dragon pattern.

Dish in blue Court Dragon pattern.

Dish in brown Court Dragon pattern.

Set of eight plates, c. 1950s. Scalloped, 5⅓"
each. Court Dragon pattern in different
colors. $400.00 – 450.00.

Plate in purple Court Dragon pattern.

Plate in pink Court Dragon pattern.

Plate in black Court Dragon pattern.

Plate in green Court Dragon pattern.

Plate in yellow Court Dragon pattern.

Plate in brown Court Dragon pattern.

Plate in blue Court Dragon pattern.

Demitasse cup and saucer, c. 1950s. Cup in Royal Flute shape with twisted feather handle, 2¾" x 2⅓". Saucer, 4¼", blue Court Dragon pattern. $200.00 – 250.00.

Close-up of design on border of saucer.

Close-up of dragon.

Set in purple.

Set in brown Court Dragon pattern.

Set in pink Court Dragon pattern.

Close-up of phoenix birds.

Set in green Court Dragon pattern.

Demitasse cup and saucer, c. 1850 – 1900. Cup in Royal Flute shape, 2¾" x 2⅓". Saucer, 4¼". Yellow and brown Court Dragon pattern. $250.00 – 300.00.

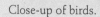

Close-up of birds.

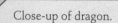

Close-up of dragon.

Coffee cup and saucer, c. 1970s. Cup in Royal Flute shape, Red Ming Dragon pattern. $200.00 – 250.00.

Three-piece smoking set, c. 1980s. Ashtray, 4½". Cigarette holder, 2¼". Candlestick, 2½". Hand-painted dragons with silver mounts. $150.00 – 200.00.

Dish, c. 1830 – 1850. Scalloped, 6". Chinoiserie design. $400.00 – 450.00.

Teapot, c. 1850 – 1900. Teapot, 5½"h, brightly decorated in Kakiemon style. $550.00 – 650.00.

Close-up of design on teapot.

Close-up of tiger.

Teacup and saucer. Meissen, c. 1970s. Cup, 3⅞" x 2". Saucer, 5¾". Derived from Meissen's famous Yellow Lion pattern portraying an orange tiger with gilt and Oriental style flowers and bamboo. $250.00 – 350.00.

Demitasse cup and saucer, c. 1850 – 1900. Cup, 2½" x 2". Saucer, 4". Unusual Indian pattern. $250.00 – 300.00.

Bowl, c. 1880s. Footed, 6½", blue and white straw flowers. $300.00 – 325.00.

Miniature cup and saucer, c. 1855 – 1863. Quatrefoil shaped cup, 2" x 2⅓". Saucer, 2⅞" x 3¾". Oriental underglaze blue flowers with gilt. $400.00 – 450.00.

Bottom of cup showing Marcolini mark.

Cup without saucer, c. 1774 – 1817. Blue and white Chinoiserie design. $125.00 – 150.00.

Shoe, c. 1950s. Turned down scuff style, 7" x 2½", underglaze blue Oriental flowers. $275.00 – 300.00.

Shoe, c. 1950s. Turned down scuff style, 3¾" x 1½", underglaze blue Oriental flowers. $175.00 – 200.00.

Breakfast cup and saucer, c. 1850s. Royal Flute shape, 4⅔" x 3". Saucer, 6⅔". Oriental flowers in blue underglaze. $175.00 – 200.00.

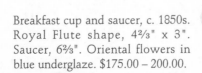

Meissen's Blue Onion pattern has endured for over 250 years and is Meissen's best known pattern. It has been copied by more companies than any other ceramic pattern in history. Many collectors agree that a piece of Blue Onion made by Meissen stands apart from its competitors'. This is due to the meticulous hand work by which each piece is made and decorated. Anyone who visits the Meissen manufactory and sees first-hand the magical transformation of a lump of wet clay into a piece of brilliant white porcelain with the lovely blue decoration will agree that Meissen Blue Onion dinnerware is the finest in the world.

Blue Onion pattern, 1984 postcard from Meissen Museum, courtesy of Meissen.

History

Blue and white porcelain from the Orient was very much in demand in Europe at the turn of the eighteenth century. After the East India Companies had established a flourishing trade with China, the Chinese quickly adapted to the European craze for blue and white porcelain.

In 1710 Augustus the Strong demanded that his new porcelain company produce blue underglaze decorations like those of the Chinese. Böttger experimented with cobalt by trial and error, but there were two problems he couldn't overcome. First, cobalt compounds reacted as flux on porcelain and tended to flow and muddle the contour of the decorations. Secondly, because of high firing temperatures, the blue paint was easily discolored.

An early associate of Böttger, David Kòhler, finally discovered the secret of the blue paint. He found that the blue paint stayed better on a new paste which contained feldspar and less alabaster. He developed new glazes containing feldspar, and he also added kaolin to the paint. These changes were the stabilizing factors for the blue underglaze paint and were used by Höroldt, the famous color chemist and painter at the Meissen manufactory.

Blue Onion, or Zwielbelmuster, was created in 1739 after Höroldt had perfected the blue underglaze paint. The model for the pattern was probably a flat bowl from the Chinese K'ang Hsi period (1662 – 1722), which is now on display at the Meissen Museum.

Decoration

The fruits are not onions but made to resemble Chinese peaches and pomegranates. In the original East Asian decoration the peach was the symbol of longevity, and the pomegranate represented fertility. Both of these fruits were popular in Europe in the seventeenth and eighteenth centuries and were grown in court gardens. The flower in the design is a cross between a peony and a chrysanthemum. The elements in the center of the pattern are the bamboo trunk, blossom, and leaves.

The Blue Onion pattern is characterized by a dominant geometrical configuration consisting of the circle, the octagon, and the square. These shapes symbolize models of being. The Onion pattern was produced at a time when artists worked predominantly with allegorical and symbolic image concepts, when all colors, plants, animals, and geometrical figures had certain spiritual meanings that very rarely exist today.

The circle is a symbol of infinity, the universe, and eternity. The square symbolizes the earth and the limited space of a human being's earthly life. It illustrates the number four, which is the number of the four elements, extending in four directions and governed by the four seasons. The octagon mediates between the circle and square and is the symbolic mediation between heaven and earth. With the octagon, the square and the circle begins in the sense of a spiritual transition from one form of being to another.

Changes

The original pattern of 1739 underwent a few changes. At first all the fruits on the border pointed inward with the stem on the edge. After a few years, the arrangement changed. The fruits began to point inward and outward alternately.

The heads of the Meissen manufactory liked the pattern because it was cheaper to produce than other decorated wares. It could be painted by lower paid "blue painters" and even by journeymen and apprentices. Also, it did not need a third firing which was necessary to fix enamel decoration, and no gilding was added to the standard ware.

During Victorian times when home furnishing became darker and heavier, the Blue Onion pattern seemed to complement this new elaborate furniture style preferred by wealthy middle classes. After 1865 the Blue Onion pattern became a craze. Tablecloths, napkins, enameled cooking pots, and utensils with the Onion pattern appeared. By the 1870s the Blue Onion pattern was adapted to fit nearly every shape produced by Meissen. Even figures were decorated in underglaze blue to complement the large Blue Onion pattern dinner, dessert, and tea services.

At the end of the nineteenth century Meissen developed a Rich Onion pattern which is a blue underglaze decoration highlighted with red and gold over the glaze. Green Onion and Red Onion patterns were also developed. Ludwig Sturm, head of the painting department at Meissen, designed a New Onion pattern. He chose different fruit and flowers and arranged them symmetrically. But it was not what people were used to and did not do well. Production of his design was finally discontinued.

Meissen dinnerware, including Blue Onion, Meissen demonstration studio.

Blue Onion Today

Underglaze cobalt painting of Blue Onion pattern, Meissen demonstration studio.

The Blue Onion pattern is still hand painted at Meissen today, just as it always has been. The painters prepare an unglazed piece by copying the outlines of the pattern on it. They use strips of tinfoil into which each painter has punched the outlines of the pattern with a pin. Through the little holes they sprinkle carbon dust onto the porcelain piece. The general idea of this method is to get the proportions of the pattern right on the piece and put each element in its proper place. The painters follow as best they can the dotted lines, but small deviations are unavoidable.

After the Blue Onion pattern has been painted, it is dipped into a glaze solution, and the decoration disappears completely under the glaze liquid.

The glaze becomes transparent during firing at 1450°C, and the beautiful cobalt blue pattern shines through.

Blue crossed swords mark on bamboo trunk.

The Most Copied Pattern

Meissen's Blue Onion pattern has been widely copied by more than 60 European, American, and Oriental factories. The Royal Porcelain Manufactory in Berlin (KPM) was one of the most serious competitors, utilizing the Onion pattern from the eighteenth to the twentieth centuries. The company used the scepter mark, and the quality of its products matched that of the Meissen factory.

Another popular producer of the Onion pattern was L. Hutschenreuther, who printed the pattern since it was produced in quantity for every day use. The pieces were marked with L. Hutschenreuther trademarks but were advertised as Meissen. Villeroy and Boch and Royal Copenhagen also copied the Blue Onion design, but gave it their own name.

The manufacture of the Onion pattern in Bohemia began in 1885 in Dubi. The original factory was acquired by Carl Teichert from the town of Meissen and was called the Meissen Stove and Fireclay Factory. The company copied the Meissen pattern exactly, hand painting its copies. In 1882 it registered a trademark with the name "Meissen," which has caused confusion to this day.

The mark is "MEISSEN" inside an oval with a star underneath.

In 1895 the Meissen Stove and Fireclay Factory was sold to Bernard Bloch, a ceramic producer and owner of a porcelain factory in Uncin, Bohemia (Czechoslovakia today). The factory is still in operation, and the Blue Onion pattern is its main product. At present, the company produces more than 5,000 Onion patterned items per day. Over half of the items are exported, many to the United States.

Blue Danube is a modern line of Onion patterned dinnerware produced in Japan and distributed by Lipper International of Wallingford, Connecticut. Over 125 items are available and are sold in most large department stores.

Some of the European manufacturers produced Blue Onion stoneware in addition to their porcelain examples. Since the pattern wasn't copyrighted, it could be used by anyone. To protect the actual Meissen pieces, the company put the famous blue crossed swords mark at the foot of the bamboo trunk in the design in 1888. Meissen Blue Onion pieces without this mark date before 1888.

Covered jam pot with attached underplate, c. 1950s. 6½" x 4½", rose finial on lid, Blue Onion pattern. $175.00 – 200.00.

Bell, c. 1930s. 4½", Blue Onion pattern. $100.00 – 125.00.

Knife rest, c. 1850 – 1887. 3¾", Blue Onion pattern. $90.00 – 100.00.

Serving bowl, c. 1888 – 1924.
Open work border, 9½",
Blue Onion pattern.
$350.00 – 400.00.

Teacup and saucer, c. 1865 – 1887.
Blue Onion with gilt rims,
$150.00 – 175.00.

Another view of above serving bowl.

Demitasse cup and saucer, c. 1860 – 1924.
Cup in Royal Flute shape with divided
feather handle, Blue Onion pattern.
$85.00 – 100.00.

Turkey platter, c.
1860 – 1887. Large,
23" x 18", Blue Onion
pattern with gilt trim.
$800.00 – 900.00.

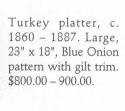

Demitasse cup and saucer. Meissen, c. 1930s,
two incised marks. Quatrefoil shaped
cup, 3¼"w x 2"h. Saucer, 4⅞".
Blue Onion pattern.
$75.00 – 100.00.

Plate, c. 1887 – 1924.
Scalloped, 6¾", Rich Onion pattern, red
and blue fruits and flowers with gilt.
$75.00 – 100.00.

Underplate/platter, c. 1930s.
Curled shape, 13½" x 9", Blue Onion
pattern, originally used as an underplate for a tureen.
$375.00 – 400.00.

Plate, c. 1888 – 1924.
Reticulated border, 9½",
Blue Onion pattern.
$350.00 – 400.00.

Another view of above platter.

Demitasse cup and saucer, c. 1950s. Royal Flute cup with entwined leaf handle, 2½"w x 1¾". Saucer, 4¼", Rich Onion pattern. $175.00 – 200.00.

Crossed swords mark in bamboo trunk.

Covered bowl, c. 1930s. Twisted feather finial on lid, 8½" x 4½", vivid Blue Onion pattern. $300.00 – 350.00.

Figural centerpiece, c. 1850 – 1887. Two-tier, swirled, with reticulated borders, figure of little boy, Blue Onion pattern with gilt. $1,500.00 – 1,900.00.

Another view of above bowl.

Coffee cup and saucer, c. 1900. Scalloped cup with curled loop handle, Blue Onion pattern. $100.00 – 125.00.

Coffee cup and saucer, c. 1850 – 1887. Royal Flute cup with twisted feather handle, Blue Onion pattern. $100.00 – 125.00.

Mismatched demitasse cup and saucer, c. 1888 – 1924. Cup in Royal Flute shape, quatrefoil saucer, Blue Onion pattern. $50.00 – 75.00.

Dessert plate, c. 1888 – 1924. New Cutout, 7¾", Blue Onion pattern. $75.00 – 100.00.

Luncheon plate, c. 1888 – 1924. Scalloped, reticulated border, 8¾", Blue Onion pattern. $175.00 – 200.00.

Teacup and saucer, c. 1934 – 1935. Cup, 3⅓" x 1¾". Saucer, 5¾".
Rich Onion pattern. $150.00 – 200.00.

Dessert plate, c. 1850 – 1880. Reticulated, 7¾",
three floral cartouches on border, Blue Onion
pattern. $150.00 – 200.00.

Bowl, c. 1888 – 1924. Reticulated, 9¼", Blue Onion pattern.
$375.00 – 400.00.

Close-up of floral cartouche on above dessert plate.

Set of eight dessert plates,
c. 1850 – 1887. New
Cutout, 7¼", Blue Onion
pattern. $500.00 – 700.00.

Set of 10 dinner plates, c. 1850 – 1880.
Reticulated, 9½" each, Blue Onion pattern.
$1,700.00 – 2,000.00.

Single plate from set of 10.

Candy dish, c. 1950s.
Three curled feet and rolled handle,
4⅓" x 2¼", Blue Onion pattern.
$100.00 – 150.00.

Another view.

Serving bowl, c. 1850 –
1887. Square, 9", Blue
Onion pattern with
gilt. $350.00 – 400.00.

Platter, c. 1850 – 1887.
Round, 12", Blue Onion
pattern with gilt rim.
$500.00 – 600.00.

Meat platter, c. 1850 – 1887. 22" long, Blue Onion pattern with gilt rim.
$800.00 – 1,000.00.

Compote, c.
1850 – 1887.
Reticulated,
footed, 9"h,
Blue Onion
pattern with
gilt. $700.00
– 800.00.

Coffee cup and saucer, c. 1935 – 1950, two incised
marks. Footed, scalloped cup, 3⅛" x 2½".
Saucer, 5½". Blue Onion pattern.
$60.00 – 75.00.

Plate, c. 1850 – 1887. Unusual border, 8½", Blue Onion pattern. $125.00 – 150.00.

Pair of candlesticks, c. 1950s. 6" each, Blue Onion pattern. $300.00 – 350.00.

Egg cup, c. 1924 – 1934. Small, scalloped, Blue Onion pattern. $75.00 – 100.00

Demitasse pot, c. 1950s, two incised marks. 6½", rose finial, Blue Onion pattern. $250.00 – 300.00.

Close-up of Meissen crossed swords mark in bamboo trunk.

Plate, c. 1888 – 1924.
8½", reticulated border,
Blue Onion pattern.
$175.00 – 200.00.

Plate, c. 1930s.
New Cutout, 6¾",
Blue Onion pattern.
$50.00 – 75.00.

Plate, c. 1850 – 1887.
6¾", reticulated border,
Blue Onion pattern.
$150.00 – 175.00.

Serving bowl, c. 1850 – 1887. Square,
7", Blue Onion pattern with gilt.
$250.00 – 300.00.

Serving bowl, c. 1930s.
Square, 8½", Blue Onion pattern.
$200.00 – 250.00.

Serving bowl, c. 1850 – 1887. 8½",
Square, Blue Onion pattern with gilt.
$350.00 – 400.00.

Coffee cup, c. 1850 – 1887.
Lobed, quatrefoil-shaped
cup, Blue Onion pattern.
$40.00 – 50.00.

Demitasse cup and saucer,
c. 1930s. Quatrefoil-shaped
cup with Dresden handle,
Blue Onion pattern.
$75.00 – 100.00.

Platter, c. 1950s. 16½", Blue Onion pattern.
$400.00 – 450.00.

Demitasse cup and saucer, c. 1930s.
Cup, 2½" x 2". Saucer, 4¼". Rich
Onion pattern. $175.00 – 200.00.

Close-up of cup.

Egg cup, c. 1888 – 1924.
4", Blue Onion pattern.
$100.00 – 150.00.

Cream pitcher, c. 1888 – 1924.
5¼", Blue Onion pattern.
$75.00 – 100.00.

Demitasse cup and saucer, c. 1850 – 1887. Royal
Flute cup, Blue Onion pattern. $125.00 – 150.00.

Ashtray, c. 1950s. 5", Blue Onion pattern.
$50.00 – 60.00.

Coaster, c. 1970s. 4", Blue Onion pattern.
$25.00 – 30.00.

Gold ornamentation has been used to enhance fine porcelain since the early Oriental wares were imported into Europe in the seventeenth century. In their comprehensive book *Porcelain of the Nineteenth Century*, Fay-Halle and Mundt emphasize the importance of gilding. "The quality of a factory's product is dependent on the quality of its gilded decoration which gives the pieces their character." This is what separates Meissen from all the other manufacturers; its gilding is second to none. Gilding is what makes Meissen unique.

In 1717 Böttger discovered a usable process for the application of a gold decoration. It was a fulminating gold solution that under certain conditions exploded. On porcelain, this gold looked like a pinkish luster similar to mother-of-pearl. This was not an acceptable gilding process for Meissen.

Meissen experimented with a variety of methods of gilding in the eighteenth century:

Japanned – This method used gold leaf which was applied to the glaze using gum Arabic and after firing was burnished, forming a thin layer of bright gold.

Honey – Many factories of the eighteenth century mixed gold leaf powder with oil of lavender and honey and applied the mixture to the porcelain with a brush, building up layers which could then be chased.

Mercury – In the late eighteenth century, a technique evolved whereby gold leaf powder was mixed with mercury and applied to the porcelain with a brush. The mercury vaporized in firing, leaving a film of gold which could then be burnished to a brassy, bright finish. This technique allowed rapid decoration and was suitable for use with a stencil, making it a popular method for large dinner services.

Meissen, along with many other manufacturers, tried to develop less expensive methods of gilding, such as the use of gold transfer prints, painting with liquid gold, and the application of a paste after engine firing and then gilding and burnishing.

Gilding came into its own at the beginning of the nineteenth century when George Kersting was appointed head of Meissen's painting department. He improved the light gilding by using a different adhesive medium to fix the gold preparation to the glaze by using oil and turpentine. This new gilding method saved Meissen large amounts of gold. This was necessary after the Napoleonic Wars as it was more efficient and cheaper.

When Heinrich Kühn became the technical manager at Meissen, he came up with triangle gilding that used a smaller amount of gold. It also needed polishing although it had a lower content of gold. Meissen pieces marked with a triangle had to be fired at a higher temperature.

In 1830 Kühn finally came through with his invention of luster gilding. The method had several advantages, not only because it used less gold but also when it came out of the kilns, it was already shiny and did not require polishing. Luster gold is still being used at Meissen. This method has never been able to match the qualities of the heavy gilding which Meissen uses for more valuable items.

This heavy or raised gilt decoration is intended to simulate the effect of jeweling. To create the pattern, the decorator paints a design on the surface using a thick enamel paste. After several layers of enamel have been applied, fine gold is painted over the raised enamel in order to give the appearance of solid gold. The raised enamel is usually yellow, which helps to make it less obtrusive as the gold becomes worn, and the enamel underneath shows through.

When gold is fired, it has a dull, matte surface. Careful polishing using agate bloodstone or metal tools gives gilded surfaces a brilliant appearance. Burnished gold has a rich soft color. It is a method of polishing gilded surfaces by applying friction with a hard tool made of agate to create a luster.

As the finishing touch, the gold painter decorates the porcelain piece with paint made from metals, usually gold. This work is done at Meissen after the piece has been decorated. The gold painter supplies the embellishments, which range from a simple border to elaborate edges and framing of crests depending on the piece being produced.

The gold painters' tools are various brushes, usually made from camel, squirrel, or mink hair, depending on the desired effect. At Meissen the paint most frequently used is liquid polishing gold. After firing in the kiln, it has a dull sheen which requires polishing. Polishing tools include an agate stylus, brushes with glazed bristles, or quartz sand.

Another gold preparation with quite different characteristics is gold foil which leaves the firing process with a shiny surface. The choice of materials depends on the individual decorator and the object to be made. Sometimes different materials are used in combination with each other.

Meissen used gilding as an embellishment or to accent a piece. Gilding can be very dramatic when used with cobalt as a decoration. Cobalt, white and gold is an extremely popular color combination at Meissen. Some Meissen pieces have different shades of gilding for a dramatic contrast, such as a bright gold, dull gold, and a dark shade of gold. Many finials, handles, and spouts are embellished with gilding. Meissen dinnerware items with gold decoration are always more expensive than the same dinnerware pattern without gold.

Plate, c. 1850 – 1900. Intricately molded plate with scallop shell motif, 10", all gold, minor wear. $300.00 – 350.00.

Show plate, c. 1830 – 1850. 2½" gold border with an ornate relief design, 11", white flowers and leaves in relief in center on a pink beaded ground. $450.00 – 500.00.

Plate, c. 1927. Swirled plate, 8¾", heavy gold and white. $200.00 – 250.00.

Coffee cup, saucer, and dessert plate, c. 1924 – 1934. Footed cup with loop handle, 4"w x 2½"h. Saucer, 5¾". Dessert plate, 7¼", heavy gold leaves on white. $300.00 – 350.00.

Coffee cup and saucer, c. 1930s. Cup with curled handle, gold band inside cup, molded pink and gold decoration. $200.00 – 225.00.

Plate, c. 1850 – 1900. Swirled, 9", gold and white, some gilt wear in center cartouches. $150.00 – 175.00.

Teapot, c. 1850 – 1924. Dragon spout, 6½" x 7½", heavy gold decoration on cobalt and white. $300.00 – 350.00.

Close-up of gilt finial.

Coffee cup and saucer, c. 1860 – 1875. Shell motif in relief, pearlized pink and white on pale green, gold embellishment, gold band inside rim of cup very worn. $200.00 – 250.00.

Charger, c. 1890s. Scalloped plate with leafy motif in heavy gold bronze gilt, 12¼". $350.00 – 400.00.

Demitasse cup and saucer, c. 1850 – 1924. Slightly flared, footed cup, loop handle with flat thumb rest, cobalt with gilt molded leaf design. $250.00 – 300.00.

Demitasse cup and saucer, c. 1934 – 1950s. Scalloped footed cup with ornate gilt handle, heavy gilt decoration on cobalt and white. $275.00 – 300.00.

Coffee set, c. 1840 – 1850. Set includes coffeepot in Biedermeier style and four cups and saucers, gilt relief floral decoration. $900.00 – 1,000.00.

Coffee cup and saucer, c. 1850 – 1900. Footed cup and saucer with molded leaves with gilt, some wear on heavy gilt band inside cup, touch of cobalt on rim. $150.00 – 200.00.

Coffee cup and saucer, c. 1850 – 1924. Footed cup with gilt broken loop handle, heavy gilt decoration on white. $200.00 – 250.00.

Same as above set in demitasse size. $200.00 – 250.00.

Covered box, c. 1850 – 1900. Hinged, in heart shape, 3" x 2¾", gilt and white flowers on yellow ground. $250.00 – 275.00.

Bottom of box.

Coffee cup and saucer, c. 1850 – 1900. Footed cup with heavy gold band inside, 4" x 2¾". Saucer, 6". Dark red ground with heavy gold relief painting. $500.00 – 600.00.

Close-up of gilding.

Coffee cup and saucer, c. 1930s. Cup and saucer with cobalt and
gold decoration. $250.00 – 300.00.

Close-up of gilding.

Demitasse cup and saucer, c. 1924 – 1934.
Can-shaped cup with square handle, gold
interior, 2¾" x 2⅓". Saucer, 4¼",
cobalt blue. $175.00 – 200.00.

Charger, c. 1924 – 1934. 11¼",
rich cobalt blue ground with
lavish gold grapes and leaves.
. $500.00 – 600.00.

Demitasse cup and saucer, c. 1950 – 1960, two incised marks. Cup, 3" x 2". Saucer, 4¾". Gold leafy border on white. $100.00 – 125.00.

Bowl, c. 1850 – 1924. 11¼", gold scrolls and grape leaves on white. $400.00 – 500.00.

Close-up of gilding.

Coffee cup and saucer, c. 1930s. Cup with swan handle, gold interior, 2⅞" x 3". Saucer, 5¼". Peach ground. $250.00 – 300.00.

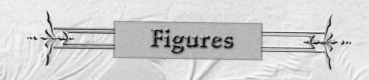

"There is probably no group of antiques so universally recognized as classics as Meissen figures, not only by collectors and dealers but by the general public...In any museum display they draw admiring crowds." (William Rogers, "The Porcelain Figures of Meissen," *Antique Trader Annual of Articles of Antiques,* 1977)

The first figures made at Meissen were the huge animals commissioned by Augustus the Strong for his Japanese Palace. Soon the manufactory realized that there was no market for these large unwieldy pieces, and smaller figures were designed. The Meissen artists found that the new porcelain material was of wonderful plasticity in its raw or green condition and very well suited to figure modeling.

It was the custom in the early eighteenth century for tables of wealthy households to be set with decorative figural centerpieces made of wax or sugar. These decorations were soon replaced with small Meissen porcelain figures. These figures decorated the cabinets and dinner tables of the aristocracy, amusing guests since many of the figures were reflections of the court society in miniature.

With the reign of Louis XV in France (1715 – 1774), the carefree Rococo movement spread to Germany. It influenced figural art at Meissen, and this period is considered the manufactory's best since porcelain matched the Rococo style perfectly.

Through the years Meissen always pulled a considerable number of figures from the same molds. Figures were not considered untouchable once they were designed. They underwent alterations and were changed when designers came up with new ideas.

Today 15% of Meissen's inventory is figures. Many are as popular today as they were in the eighteenth century. Famous series still being made today are the Italian Comedy Series, Gardening Children, Traders, Cupids, the Monkey Band, and many more.

Famous Figure Modelers

Johann Gottlieb Kirchner

Kirchner was Meissen's first figure sculptor. He had been trained as a stone and wood sculptor and became a model master in 1731. Augustus the Strong commissioned a series of large statues and animals for his Japanese Palace. Kirchner's inspiration for the pieces he designed came from Chinese porcelain and sandstone figures of animals.

Kirchner never liked working with porcelain, he preferred working with wood. In spite of his dislike of porcelain, he made the first important figures in the Meissen manufactory. Kirchner had problems with his new modeler Kaendler. Tension arose between the two men because Kirchner frequently lost his temper and was often absent from work. It was said that he realized Kaendler had superior talent and was very jealous of him. Kirchner resigned in 1733.

Johann Joachim Kaendler

After Kirchner resigned, Kaendler became Chief Modeler for Meissen in 1733 and soon gained the reputation as the "Michelangelo of his craft." His designs were inspired by mythology, music, poetry, works of art, and passing scenes. He created the Italian Comedy figures, pastoral figures, and groups satirizing court manners. His bulky crinoline skirt became an important element in early Meissen figures.

In 1764 Kaendler wrote to the Princess-Mother Electress: "On my entry into the porcelain factory in 1731, I found no figure, no piece that had been treated realistically and with skill. I at once engaged 60 workers and potters and taught them designing and adjusting without exhausting myself. Thanks to my efforts, they became artists."

Johann Friedrich Eberlein

Eberlein joined Meissen in 1735 as an assistant to Kaendler. He made large animals for the Japanese Palace and also created numerous figures and groups. His figures are easily recognized by their almond-shaped eyes, half-closed eyelids, and pointed chins. Most of his figures had long fine hands and feet.

Michel Victor Acier

Acier worked for Meissen from 1764 to 1780. His figures were more precise and consistently modeled than those of Kaendler. Many had moralizing themes. Today they are referred to as Motto figures. Most well known are his cupids, which represented the values and ideals of the eighteenth century.

Smoothing, polishing, and preparing joints of multi-part figures by a bossierer at the Meissen demonstration studio.

Paul Scheurich

Scheurich was considered the greatest figure modeler in Meissen since Kaendler. He was born in New York in 1883 and moved to Berlin in 1900. He became well known as a graphic artist and designer of theater sets and costumes. Scheurich began modeling for Meissen in 1913 and produced more than 100 models in the 20 years under Max Pfeiffer.

Scheurich loved the theater, and his early models were inspired by the Russian ballet's visit to Berlin in 1912. His ballet figures captured the dancers' movements and grace and were his best known work. As many as 1,700 Russian Ballet figures were sold between 1918 and 1924, making these the most popular of Meissen's figures. Scheurich also created figures from the Italian Comedy. When questioned about his work, Scheurich said, "At Meissen I enjoyed artistic freedom for my work with a free choice of themes and designs. Pfeiffer was very committed to my work!"

Scheurich was fired by the Nazis in 1933. He stayed in Berlin through the war. A single bombing raid destroyed his home, studio, and most of his designs. Scheurich died in 1945.

Ernst August Leuteritz

As head of the modeling department in the nineteenth century, Leuteritz refurbished and remodeled nearly all the figures made by Kaendler and his contemporaries. They included crinoline groups, Italian comedy figures, and mythological groups, as well as some animals. His production standards were very strict. He did not allow firing cracks, glaze bubbles, or any manufacturing defects. As a result, the remodeled pieces often seemed stiff. The bases had more flowers, and the faces of the figures were more doll-like than the eighteenth century pieces. Other differences were in the colors. Leuteritz used pinks, greens, brown, chrome green, and maroon. The bottom of these redesigned pieces had impressed mold numbers.

Max Esser

Esser created new and interesting animals from 1920 to 1937 and greatly enriched Meissen's inventory of sculptures. He had a studio of his own in the manufactory so that as a freelance artist he had ideal conditions for working with porcelain and fine brown stoneware. His animal sculpture Otter won a Grand Prix at the 1937 World Exposition in Paris. He designed a table service showing the fable of Reynard the Fox. His Seagull, skimming a wave in flight, has become one of Meissen's most popular pieces. Esser made monumental animal masks — big cats, apes, rams, and bears in dark Böttger stoneware.

Erich Hösel

Hösel was considered one of the most talented sculptors of his generation. He modeled many realistic animals for Meissen in natural and graceful poses. He became head of the modeling department in 1903. Hösel encouraged artists and modelers to study nature and to travel abroad for new ideas. He restored eighteenth century models to their original shapes.

Meissen bossierer working on arm.

Famous Series

Court Life

Members of the eighteenth century aristocracy in Germany were greatly influenced by the French Court. Their favorite pastimes were hunting, masquerades, and the theater. These customs were brought to life by the art of French painter Jean Antoine Watteau (1684 – 1721). His genre of painting was called Fetes Galantes — the use of delicate colors with emphasis on the courtly culture. Watteau's characters danced, laughed, sang, and were always on the lookout for amorous adventures.

Kaendler was influenced greatly by Watteau's works, evident in his famous Crinoline groups from 1740. Ladies portrayed in the crinoline dresses of the period were courted by gentlemen in

Meissen court life figure group, Meissen Exhibition Hall.

fashionable attire, often attended by Blackamoor servants. Kaendler's Crinoline groups express romantic gestures of tenderness. The embraces and clasped hands were all signs of love but above all they were expressions of eighteenth century sentiment.

Meissen sculptor Friedrich Elias Meyer (1723 – 1785) was also influenced by Watteau's paintings and created Meissen figures after 1750. His 15-piece Gallant Orchestra was characterized by delicate limbs and gracefulness. The group included a conductor, flutist, bassoon player, trumpeter, six other musicians, four flirtatious female singers, and one male singer. These figures are still being made today.

Italian Comedy

Italian Comedy, Commedia dell Arte, was a humorous theatrical production performed by professional actors who traveled throughout Italy in the sixteenth century. Performances were conducted on temporary stages, on city streets, and in open fields. The better troupes performed in palaces and became internationally known. The performances included witty dialogue, music, dance, and all kinds of trickery. The actors wore masks and therefore projected their characters' emotions through gestures, leaps, falls, and slapstick antics. This art form spread throughout Europe.

In 1744 Kaendler produced a series of exceptional Italian Comedy figures. The most frequently portrayed character is Harlequin or Arlecchino. He was modeled by Kaendler in a variety of attitudes and poses. Another successful character was the Avvocato (Lawyer) wearing a bright red or yellow gown. The Italian Comedy series is still being produced today.

In his excellent book *Meissen Porcelain*, Hallwag writes, "The Meissen crinoline and comedy group figures are among the most perfect works created by artists in china of all time. Kaendler's groups, which are extremely original and masterpieces of creative imagination, betray no sign of foreign influence. In the beginning the colors are remarkable for their freshness and for their brilliancy."

Country Life

The art of gardening flourished in the eighteenth century. During his reign, Augustus the Strong had many parks and gardens laid out in the style of French gardens. His passion for gardens is reflected in the rural subject matter of the figures created in Meissen porcelain.

Many of Meissen's pastoral groups were inspired from drawings by artists such as François Boucher. They included a shepherd playing a flute and a dancing shepherdess. A famous figure group, entitled Listener at the Well, was taken from one of Boucher's drawings. It portrays a shepherdess and cavalier making a rope of flowers with a listener eavesdropping behind the wall.

Meissen's earliest peasants and shepherds were made in the Baroque style. They were dynamic and full of vitality and depicted the harsh realities of peasant life in the eighteenth century. During the Rococo movement, this honest portrayal of country life gave way to a more romanticized depiction of rural life.

In the late eighteenth century under Marcolini, the Neoclassical movement gained momentum. The peasants had the same themes but different ornamentation. The smooth flowing lines gave way to precision and symmetry. Floral garlands were replaced by ancient Greek and Roman symbols, such as the ram's head and laurel leaf.

Children

Children were always favorite subjects of Meissen figure modelers, and several popular series were created. In the eighteenth century children were dressed as adults and shown in adult poses.

Kaendler sculpted a series of Gardening Children in the 1740s. The set included 40 pairs of children ranging from 4½" to 6½" high. They were portrayed on rocaille bases highlighted in gold. In most of the pairs, one partner's actions complemented the other. The boys are watering flowers or digging, and the girls are picking flowers or carrying bouquets. As wine growing was popular in the Elbe Valley, some of the children are picking grapes or carrying them in baskets. The Gardening Children are still being made today.

Acier produced 12 pairs of Gardening Children in 1778. They ranged in height from 4¾" to 5½" with square bases with gold bands. The figures hold gardening tools, flowers, grapes, farm animals, or musical instruments. Acier and Kaendler's children both represented an idealized version of life in an agricultural society.

Two of three Hentschel children, special limited edition series 2004 (authors' personal collection).

One of three Hentschel children, special limited edition series 2004 (authors' personal collection).

Two Meissen figures often seen in books and museums are busts of a little boy and girl. They were modeled by Kaendler in 1753 and are 9" high. They were the only figures produced at Meissen in the eighteenth century with blue eyes. They were modeled after the grandchildren of Augustus III, Prince Louis Charles de Bourbon, and Princess Maria Zepherine de Bourbon. The prince died at the age of nine of tubercular bone disease. He was the favorite of his parents and although they had 12 children, it was said they died of broken hearts a few years after his death.

There were changes in the attitude toward children after 1900. Child figures became more life-like. Children were no longer viewed as miniature adults but were depicted as independent little personalities. Julius Konrad Hentschel (1872 – 1907) created 14 porcelain children between 1904 and 1907. They were loving observations of children's activities, free from sentimentality. Some examples are children drinking, reading books, riding hobby horses, and playing with pets. Hentschel children are very popular with collectors and are still being produced today.

Street Traders

In the seventeenth and eighteenth centuries large European cities were filled with men and women vendors calling out their wares in a jargon that had come down almost unchanged since the Middle Ages. Their cries were in the form of songs and nursery rhymes, and they moved from house to house loudly hawking their wares.

A number of artists chose them as subjects for their drawings and engravings, and they were used by Meissen to develop several popular Street Trader series. Kaendler was inspired by the prints of the Comte de Caylus and created the Paris Criers with the assistance of Peter Reinicke and Johann Eberlein. Examples include a pancake seller, map seller, oysterman, poultry vendor, and lottery ticket seller urging shoppers to try their luck. The small figures were about 5" high and decorated in delicate pastel colors with gilt scrolled bases. Some of the figures were wearing shoes, but most have sabots or clogs which were cheaper and easier to wear on the cobbled streets of Paris.

For his series of London Traders, Kaendler was inspired by the engravings of Pierce Tempest after Captain Marcellus Laroon's drawings. Laroon was a Dutch painter who lived in London and specialized in street scenes.

The Russian Traders were loosely adapted from engravings by Jean-Baptiste Le Prince, a student of Boucher, who went to Russia to record the costumes and ways of the Russian people in the eighteenth century.

Cupids

Cupids and cherubs were popular symbols used in the Romantic movement and were used as subjects by the Meissen modelers. Cupid has always played a role in the celebration of love and lovers. He is known as a mischievous, winged child, whose arrows would pierce the hearts of his victims, causing them to fall deeply in love. To the Romans he was the god of love, and his mother was Venus. In ancient Greece he was known as Eros, the young son of Aphrodite.

To my VALENTINE.

Early German cupid postcard.

groups. Most famous was the Allegory of Four Seasons. This was a popular and easily recognizable allegorical subject — spring depicted flowers, summer sheaves of wheat, fall grapes, and winter coals or fire. He created cupids disguised as mortals — an actor, a money lender, a pastry seller, and a grape picker. Some of his cupids played instruments.

The famous Motto Children were modeled by Acier with the assistance of Schönheit (1775 – 1778). They were influenced by the drawings of Johannes Elias Zessig, known as Schenau. Each figure was under 6" and was inscribed in French with a motto which was interpreted by the cupid. There were sixteen figures in the series. Motto Children are very popular today.

A cherub is not a cupid, although they look much the same. Cherubim are the second highest group in the celestial hierarchy. The form they take is that of putti, which is Italian for "little boys." These plump, rose-bottom male figures were used as decorative elements in both religious and mythological art. They are found either naked or with flowing, loosely tied sashes. They are frequently portrayed with hearts, flowers, or musical instruments.

Kaendler loved creating little cupids in different poses. He was the son of a clergyman and had a good education with a strong classical background. His cupids were humorously conceived and were popular in the eighteenth century, both as individual and large

Early German cupids postcard.

Artisans

The series of workmen or artisans made by Kaendler in the mid-1750s are of great interest to collectors in the twentieth century. These figures give great insight into the tools used in the eighteenth century and are of historical interest. Examples are the Blacksmith, Carpenter, Wood Turner, Seamstress, Tinker, and Cook.

There were several Miner series, as they were held in great esteem in the Saxon courts. Abundant deposits of silver, tin, iron, copper, and semi-precious stones were discovered in Saxony during the Middle Ages, and mining became an important industry and was the major reason for Saxony's wealth. In the Miner series, most figures have tools appropriate for their job. They were 8" high and set on rocaille bases. The Artisan series consisted of 18 figures representing the trades of the period.

Distant Lands

The people and customs in Asia and Africa fascinated Europeans. The Chinese were favorite subjects of Meissen artists from the beginning. Pagoda figures which were Buddha-like Oriental sages were among the first porcelain figures produced at Meissen. The figures are hollow with openings at the mouth and ears, used to burn incense and were modeled after Chinese porcelain. They were usually seated at tea or at simple meditation.

India inspired Meyer to create his male and female Malabars in two sizes. Sultans were designed in many forms, such as a Sultan Riding on a Rhinoceros. The Sultan was part of the Arabian Nights series designed by Heinz Werner in 1970.

Exhibitions were sent to Africa, and drawings were brought back showing an extremely exotic people, who were called Moors or Blackamoors. It was considered very fashionable for wealthy Europeans to dress black servants in brightly colored clothes.

1934 Meissen pagoda figure, from Kaendler, 1731, Meissen Exhibition Hall.

Bossierer painting Malabar figure, from F. E. Meyer, 1754, Meissen postcard.

Animals

Menageries were popular in the eighteenth century, and Augustus the Strong sent expeditions to Africa for exotic animals. The first figures made at the Meissen manufactory were the large porcelain animals commissioned by Augustus for his Japanese Palace. Kaendler began designing smaller animals, and a number of popular series were produced throughout the eighteenth century.

Animal sculptures enjoyed a considerable revival at Meissen shortly before and after World War I due to the designs of Meissen sculptor Paul Walther (1876 – 1933). After renowned animal sculptor August Gaul died in 1921, Meissen bought 15 of his sculptures. These were executed in stoneware and in white porcelain. The white figures have an impressed crossed swords mark and WEIFS (white).

Monkey postcard, 1904.

Monkey Band

One of the most loved figural series ever produced by Meissen is the Monkey Band, first designed by Kaendler. Monkeys were popular pets in the eighteenth century, and there were many monkey fables, widespread in the art and literature of the time. How they fought, worked, and socialized can be found in the work of the Dutch artist Terniers.

One of the most popular fables of the time was about an entertainer who with great effort succeeded in putting monkeys in clothing and had them act as humans. A scoffer threw nuts and apples at the monkeys and ruined the act. The monkeys came out of their unnatural positions and showed themselves as they really were — monkeys.

Kaendler might have based his famous Monkey Band on this fable, on paintings and copper engravings, or he may have wanted to create a caricature of court life. It was reported that one day the court musicians played so terribly that Augustus II, who was not always polite, called them monkeys.

In 1753 Kaendler created the 21 charming musicians and, together with model maker Peter Reinicke, completed them in 1765. They included a conductor, 16 musicians, and four singers. The Monkey Band immediately gained the public's affection. Shortly after its appearance it had become so popular that the English porcelain factory Chelsea copied it in 1756. Reinicke made a new version of the Monkey Band a few years later. Otto Pilz renewed the Monkey Band by Kaendler and Reinicke in a modern version from 1908 to 1912.

The Monkey Band is still being produced by Meissen, and it remains one of their most popular series. At a September 1996 William Doyle auction, a Meissen Monkey Band was estimated at $6,000 – 9,000, and it reached $18,400.

WHITETHROAT

White throat bird. English postcard,
© J. Salmon Ltd., Seven Oakes, England.

Birds

Kaendler began to create birds in porcelain as early as the 1730s. His first large commissions were intended for Augustus's Japanese Palace in Dresden. Soon after, smaller birds appropriate for cabinets and tables were being made by the manufactory.

Kaendler was a keen observer of nature. There were numerous stuffed birds in the Palace menagerie that Kaendler used as models for his creations. He made many models of exquisite birds. Most popular were the birds that were kept as pets, particularly parrots and canaries. Game birds were produced, such as pheasants and ducks. Kaendler produced song birds in vivid colors and detail. He captured typical moments in the birds' lives, for example a robin looking after her babies.

Over 30 birds are made by Meissen at the present, including the parrot, cockatoo, chaffinch, canary, peacock, rooster, great titmouse, gold finch, and robin.

Majestic Meissen eagle figure,
Meissen Factory Museum.

Pug Dog

Pug dogs were brought over to Europe from Asia by the Dutch East India Company in the late sixteenth century. Sailors obtained the lion-like dogs directly from China or Turkey and were captivated by their resemblance to the fabled Chinese Fu dogs.

The pug dog became a popular breed in the eighteenth century and was the insignia of "The Order of the Pug Dogs," a fake Freemason's Society. This organization was established because the Pope decreed that Freemasonry was to be outlawed. This distressed the Saxon aristocracy, for although they were devout Catholics, they greatly enjoyed the social aspects of Freemasonry. They therefore invented a sham society, giving it the name of their pet dog.

The pug was the favorite pet of Count Brühl, prime minister for Augustus III and director of Meissen from 1733 to 1763. The pug was one of the earliest animal figures made by Meissen, and it is still being produced today.

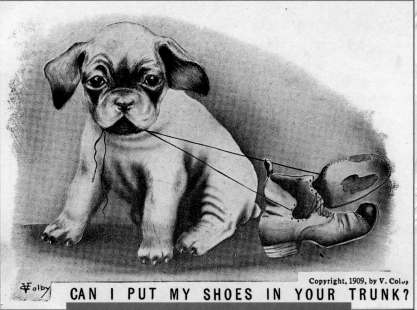

Copyright, 1909, by V. Colus,

CAN I PUT MY SHOES IN YOUR TRUNK?

"Can I put my shoes in your trunk?" by Volby.
Early postcard © 1909 V. Colus.

Figural sweetmeat dish, c. 1850 – 1900. Reclining man, 11½" x 7½", cobalt blue and gilt flowered coat, excellent facial features, possible restoration on foot. $1,200.00 – 1,350.00.

Figure group, c. 1890 – 1900. Three cupids holding flowers, 3½" x 4". $900.00 – 1,100.00.

Another view.

Figure of cupid, c. 1924 – 1934. Seated, with garland of grapes and leaves on head, 2¼"w x 3½"h, cupid squeezing grapes into wine goblet. $500.00 – 550.00.

Cupid, c. 1924 – 1934.
Seated, 2"w x 3¼"h,
holding a bouquet of flowers
in each hand, minor chip on a leaf.
$450.00 – 500.00.

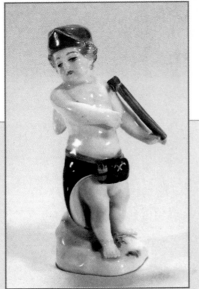

Cupid, c. 1930s. Miner, 3¾", has ax
and dagger and is wearing green hat.
$500.00 – 550.00.

Back view.

Cupid, c. 1850 – 1900. Beautifully
formed figure, 5", grape garland
around head and holding a grape
which has a break, missing end of
thumb. $400.00 – 450.00.

Gardening Boy, c. 1930 – 1950s,
sitting atop a basket of flowers,
5¼", holding a floral wreath.
$725.00 – 775.00.

Close-up of face.

Close-up of face.

Gardening Girl, c. 1930 –
1950s. Carrying basket
of roses, 5", beautifully
hand-painted dress with
coral and purple flowers.
$700.00 – 750.00.

Cupid, c. 1930s. 4", playing the violin, fur hat. $600.00 – 650.00.

Back view.

Close-up of face.

Figurine, c. 1850 – 1924. Charming girl and boy, 4½" x 6½", lovely hand-painted costumes. $1,000.00 – 1,200.00.

Back view.

Figural sweetmeat bowl, c. 1860. Reclining lady holding bowl, 7½"w x 5"h, lady with gold necklace and hand-painted costume, applied flowers on bottom of bowl. $1,800.00 – 2,000.00.

Back view.

Figure of young man, c. 1850 – 1924. Leaning against tree stump holding flute, pug dog at his feet, 6¼". $700.00 – 750.00.

Two Baker's Chocolate women, c. 1860s. Figure on left, 15" x 5¾". Figure on right, 14½" x 5¾". Hand-painted costumes. $2,000.00 – 2,500.00 each.

Figurine, c. 1860. Lady and man leaning against column holding tureen, 6"w x 10"h, exceptional modeling and hand-painted detail of costumes. $3,000.00 – 3,500.00.

Pair of busts of children, c. 1860s. Beautiful girls depicting fall and spring, 9½" each, lovely facial detail, well formed teeth. $5,500.00 – 6,000.00 pair.

Motto Child, c. 1850 – 1900. Cupid holding roses, 5½", inscribed "Je les couronne." $1,300.00 – 1,400.00.

Motto child, c. 1850 – 1900. Cupid holding up a heart, 5¾", inscribed "Je les punis." $1,300.00 – 1,400.00.

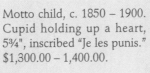

Boy feeding ducks, c. 1900. 5", $1,200.00 – 1,300.00.

Lady with basket of flowers, c. 1890. 5¼", $1,200.00 – 1,300.00.

Two young girls, c. 1890. 5" x 5½", one girl with flower lei around neck holding mask. $1,400.00 – 1,500.00.

Close-up of two girls.

Two boys under a tree, c. 1895. 7¼".
$1,800.00 – 1,900.00.

Woman with a fan, c.
1895. Aristocratic lady
with lace cuffs and collar,
holding a fan, 8½".
$1,900.00 – 2,000.00.

Man with firewood, c. 1895.
7¼", $1,800.00 – 1,900.00.

Two cupids, c. 1850 – 1900. Adorable, one asleep on a
drum, 7¼"w x 6"h. $2,400.00 – 2,500.00.

Boy with shovel, c. 1956. Gardening child, 5½", holding flower in one hand and shovel in the other. $750.00 – 850.00.

Another view.

Close-up of face.

Girl with shovel, c. 1956. Gardening child, 5½", holding flower in one hand and shovel in the other. $750.00 – 850.00.

Another view.

Pan with windmill, c. 1850 – 1900.
6½", exceptional facial expression
and skin tones. $1,200.00 – 1,300.00.

Another view.

Close-up
of face.

Lady holding basket of
grapes, c. 1850 – 1900.
May be part of Paris
Criers Tradesman group,
5¼", well painted cos-
tume and good facial
features. $900.00 –
1,000.00.

Italian Comedy child, c.
1900. Boy, 5¼", excellent
facial expression and beautifully painted costume.
$900.00 – 1,000.00.

Back view.

Close-up of face.

Close-up of face.

Girl with duck, c. 1840s. Wide brimmed pink hat, basket over shoulders with duck inside, 4¾". $800.00 – 900.00.

Another view.

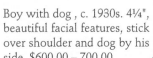

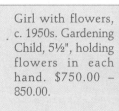

Boy with dog , c. 1930s. 4¼", beautiful facial features, stick over shoulder and dog by his side. $600.00 – 700.00.

Girl with flowers, c. 1950s. Gardening Child, 5½", holding flowers in each hand. $750.00 – 850.00.

Boy with basket of flowers, c. 1890s. 5", basket of applied flowers in one hand and a flower in the other. $700.00 – 750.00.

Close-up.

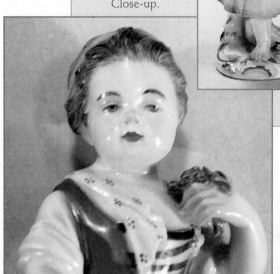

Cupid with broken heart, c. 1850 – 1900. 8½", gazing sadly at broken heart in his hands, set of arrows hanging from his waist, base simulates marble. $1,200.00 – 1,500.00.

Back view.

Figurine Sultan, c. 1970s. Designed by Peter Strang, from the Arabian Nights, 4½" x 7". Smiling Sultan perched on a blue and gilt podium. $850.00 – 950.00.

Another view.

Close-up of face.

Close-up of face.

Cupid, c. 1870s. Four Seasons figure, 5½", cupid carrying a sickle and sheaves of wheat to depict summer. $800.00 – 900.00.

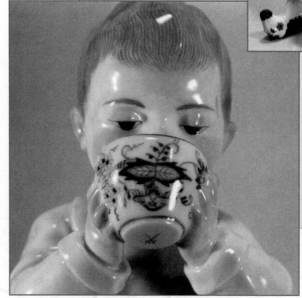

Figure Hentschel child, current mark, little boy drinking from a Blue Onion decorated cup with hobby horse dragging underneath his nightshirt, 7". $1,100.00.

Another view.

Back view.

Close-up.

Girl with Flowers, c. 1935 – 1950. Holding flowers in apron, 5¼"h, basket of flowers in left hand. $600.00 – 700.00.

Hentschel child, current mark. Little boy with expressive face riding hobby horse with newspaper hat, 7". $1,400.00.

Hentschel child, current mark. Baby, 5¼", adorable little girl with plaid jumper sitting on cushion eating a cookie. $1,500.00.

Another view.

Close-up of face.

Another view.

Cupid, c. 1850 – 1924. Holding broken heart, 5½", sad expression on face. $900.00 – 1,000.00.

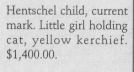

Hentschel child, current mark. Little girl holding cat, yellow kerchief. $1,400.00.

Close-up of face.

Another view.

Close-up of face.

Back view.

Hentschel child, current mark. Plaid shirt, sitting watching his dog drinking, 6" x 3½". $1,600.00.

Close-up of face.

Side view.

Cupid, c. 1850 – 1924. Mixing in bowl, 7½". $1,200.00 – 1,500.00.

Horse, c. 1930s. 5" x 7½", all white, exceptional modeling. $400.00 – 500.00.

Another view.

Calf, c. 1930 – 1950s. 3¾" x 3¼", all white. $275.00 – 300.00.

Sealyham Terrier, c. 1930s.
Red stoneware dog, 5¾"h,
nicely molded. $275.00 –
300.00.

Another view.

Close-up of face.

Pair of canaries, c. 1890s.
On tree stumps, 10"h each.
$2,000.00 – 2,200.00.

Deer, c. 1950 – 1960.
4½"w x 5"h, all white.
$250.00 – 300.00.

Rhinoceros with black Nubian boy, c. 1860s. Rhino, 9"w, all white, gilt decoration. $6,500.00 – 7,000.00.

Front view of rhinoceros.

Miniature parrot, c. 1850 – 1900. 2"h, well painted in blue, green, red, and yellow. $200.00 – 250.00.

Cardinal, c. 1950 – 1960. 4½" x 6½", beautifully modeled, all white. $350.00 – 400.00.

Canary, c. 1970. 4¼", perched on stump with applied flowers. $400.00 – 450.00.

Another view.

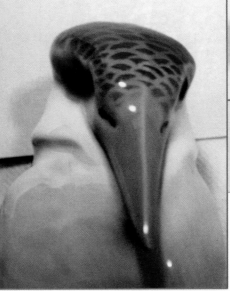

Kingfisher, c. 1850 – 1924. 5½", painted in shades of turquoise and pale pink. $600.00 – 650.00.

Another view.

Close-up of face.

Bird, c. 1962. 9"h, perched on white tree trunk, richly painted. $900.00 – 1,000.00.

Bird, c. 1924 – 1934.
Head down, 3½", green with
blue and white feathers.
$400.00 – 500.00.

Close-up
of face.

Another view.

Another view.

Oriole, c. 1950s.
6". $700.00 – 800.00.

Close-up of face.

Front view.

Chaffinch, c. 1850 – 1924. 5¾".
$600.00 – 700.00.

Close-up of face.

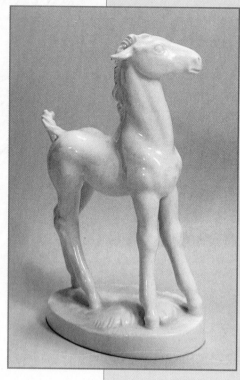

Horse, c. 1950s.
5"w x 7½"h, all white.
$400.00 – 500.00.

Another view.

Close-up of face.

Canary, c. 1850 – 1924.
3½". $400.00 – 450.00.

The beauty and value of Meissen porcelain have made it an object of desire from the beginning. Meissen porcelain was stolen, sold underhandedly, and painted outside the manufactory. Meissen designs were copied by many companies throughout Europe and England. This occurred because old and sought-after patterns belong to porcelain history and were free for all. Only decorations developed after 1919 are protected if a copyright has been obtained. Perfect Meissen painting is sometimes found on these copies. The reason for this is that painters trained at Meissen frequently left the manufactory and opened up their own shops or joined other companies.

Outside Painters

From the early 1720s there was an increasing quantity of Meissen porcelain that was decorated outside the factory. The uncertainty of the manufacturing process in the early years resulted in a high proportion of "wasters" which were sold off to outside painters or hausmalers. Today the works of the early hausmalers, especially those in Augsburg in the eighteenth century, are considered almost as valuable as Meissen painting of the time.

Thefts and smuggling of porcelain out of the Meissen manufactory were something that has never been stopped completely, even now. The reason this has been prevalent is that decorated porcelain is more expensive than white ware, and some people saw a chance to pocket the different by decorating Meissen porcelain themselves.

English Copycats

In the eighteenth century several English porcelain companies tried to copy the success of Meissen porcelain. Chelsea copied Meissen's sweetmeat dishes, pastoral figures, and the Monkey Band.

As early as 1753 Derby called its figures the "second Dresden." The company made good quality figures with lace embellishments and marked the pieces with a blue crossed mark.

In the nineteenth century, a number of firms such as Coalport and Minton used the crossed swords trademark on their Meissen style pieces. Coalport's elaborate Coalbrookdale pieces encrusted with flowers were inspired by Meissen pieces. Minton made a series of Meissen style seated figures of ladies symbolizing the five senses.

A French Copycat

Edmé Sampson operated a porcelain factory in Paris, France, in 1845. The company was owned by members of his family until 1964 when C. G. Riehar-chare took over. Sampson was known for making good quality reproductions and copies of porcelain from famous manufactories, including Meissen, and was given the title "Sampson the Imitator." Until about 1870, the company seemed only to have decorated porcelain made by other factories in their own style. Sampson copied Meissen's crossed swords mark in the nineteenth century, adding its letter "S" between the hilts. The company excelled in copying Meissen's bird figures and early Oriental pieces.

German Copycats

Dresden Porcelain Decorating Studios

At the end of the eighteenth century the Romantic movement influenced all areas of intellectual life in Germany. One of the centers of this movement was in Dresden. Artists, poets, musicians, and philosophers were attracted by the Baroque beauty of the city with its splendid collections, its charming surroundings, and the stimulating intellectual and artistic atmosphere, and moved there. Important artists made Dresden a center of the Romantic School of Painting.

In the late nineteenth century there was a considerable demand among the middle classes for porcelain and other hand-crafted objects for interior decoration at moderate prices. This demand was met by the Dresden decorating studios.

Directories from 1855 – 1944 show more than 200 painting shops in Dresden alone. Most of them employed several artists. Many shops also contracted with decorators who worked at home and were paid by the piece.

Many of the large shops had their studios near the Dresden Main-Railway Station at Prager and Zinzendorfer Streets. Many of the shops dealt in antiques and fine art, and some had their own kilns.

Large quantities of white porcelain or blanks were bought from porcelain manufacturers in Germany, Austria, and Limoges, France, by the Dresden studios for decorating, marketing and reselling throughout the world as Dresden china. Much of the white ware was ordered without marks, and the decorators applied their own marks. Because the demand for Dresden porcelain was so great, the studios sometimes had to use blanks that were already marked. The decorators hid the mark under a blob of gold paint or under a gold flower blossom. The size and shape of the blossom depended on the size and shape of the original porcelain manufacturer's mark. A Dresden style came into being which was a mixture of Meissen and Vienna flower and figure painting.

HELENA WOLFSOHN

The earliest Dresden studio to copy Meissen's designs was Helena Wolfsohn who began operation in 1843. During the period 1875 – 1915 there were 30 painters working at the studio. After Helena Wolfsohn's death, the business was continued by her daughter, Madame Elb, and then by her son. In 1919 Walter Ernst Stephan took over, but little is known of the late production.

Helena Wolfsohn used various forms of "A R" in script from 1843 to 1883. This mark was similar to the early Meissen mark. The A R monogram was officially registered with British trademarks in July 1877, in the name of Helena Wolfsohn, a widow. The supporting statement was made that the firm used the mark for 34 years. As the A R mark is usually found under the glaze, it can be assumed that Wolfsohn ordered it placed on the production of the porcelain itself, before the glaze firing process.

In 1879 Meissen took Wolfsohn to court regarding the use of the A R mark. Wolfsohn won, and Meissen appealed it. It was overturned in 1881. At this time the firm adopted a mark using a crown with the letter "D" underneath. Wolfsohn also used the word Dresden, surmounted by a crown. The gold overglaze flower mark was used from 1880 to 1945 to cover the manufacturer's mark.

Wolfsohn purchased white china blanks from the Meissen factory and had them decorated by her own staff of painters and gilders.

The workshop of Helena Wolfsohn was one of the most prolific decorating studios in Dresden. It specialized in painting vases and tea and coffee wares. The decoration was typically divided into quarters with figures decorated in the Watteau style alternating with flowers on rich ground colors.

The company did some fine quality large vases and ginger jars during the A R period, 1850 – 1870. These items were painted with delicate Chinese scenes, birds, and battle scenes modeled after eighteenth century Meissen patterns. Simple gilt borders on a fish-scale design were used. The vases were often in the form of long-necked bottles or in the double gourd shape. Some were embellished with goat's head handles or masks at the sides.

Dessert services were painted in the Meissen style with fruit, birds, landscapes, and sea views. Plates often had reticulated or basketweave borders. Highly decorative objects such as vases and urns had cupids *en camaieu* (monochrome painting), or subjects from Teniers, Van Ostade, Hogarth, and other artists.

CARL THIEME

Carl Thieme was possibly one of the best copycats of Meissen porcelain. He started a china decorating studio in Potschappel, Germany, in 1867. The town is located in eastern Germany in the state of Saxony between the foothills of the Erzgebirge Mountains, ten miles from Dresden. In 1921 the town was combined with the villages of Deuben and Doehlen to form the city of Freital.

Thieme's studio decorated porcelain white ware bought from the C. G. Schierholz factory in Plaue, Saxony, in the Meissen and Vienna styles. On October 2, 1872, the company began producing its own porcelain and was named Saxon Porcelain Manufactory Dresden. One of the frequently used marks from 1888 to 1901 was crossed lines with a "T" in underglaze or overglaze blue or black.

The company openly copied Meissen, Vienna, and Sevres forms, figures, and decoration. They copied Meissen's famous busts of children, the Gardening Children, and cupids in many forms. Many of its decorative pieces were embellished with applied flowers in the Meissen style.

In 1909 Thieme made a group of figures that were copies of Meissen's famous crinoline and harlequin figures designed by Kaendler, c. 1730 – 1760. A group of unscrupulous London dealers sold the Thieme porcelains as "Old Dresden" (Meissen) and became involved in a lawsuit. It is reported that Charles Dickens was swindled by these dealers. It took experts to determine that the pieces were not genuine Meissen figures. The Danish ceramic expert Hannover said, "Of the works in Saxony at the present imitating old Meissen porcelain, the cleverest and most dangerous is probably the Sachische Porzellafabrik Carl Thieme."

There were many quarrels between the Meissen and Thieme companies, some of them taken to courts. Thieme's early marks, various forms of crossed lines with the letter "T," were criticized by Meissen who thought the marks were too close to their famous crossed swords mark. Thieme promised not to use the mark and declared its intention to mark its porcelain with the letters "S.P.F." (Saxonian Porcelain Factory) in script, which it did in 1901. The word "Dresden" was included below the letters as the names "Dresden" and "Dresden china" were not protected.

The bickering between Thieme and other Dresden studios with Meissen continued for years. In December 1930 representatives from Meissen, C. M. Hutschenreuther, several Dresden porcelain studios, and the Thieme factory came to an agreement. Meissen declared that it would not object to the use of "Dresden china" by the others, and they were allowed to call themselves producers of Dresden china. All of them promised to enforce the agreement against anyone outside of their group.

After World War II a court decision ruled on the Dresden matter once and for all. Only a studio or company physically doing business in a certain city was allowed to use the name of the city in its advertising or trademark. For Meissen, this meant the end of the use of the name Dresden or Dresden china for its porcelains. For the Carl Thieme Company this meant it could legally include Dresden it its name because Freital had been legally incorporated into the city of Dresden.

FRANZISKA HIRSCH

Franziska Hirsch operated a porcelain studio on Struwestrasse 19 in Dresden from 1894 to 1930, decorating in the Meissen and Vienna styles. The company's early marks were variations of crossed lines or staffs and the initial "H" in overglaze blue.

In 1896 Meissen successfully won a lawsuit against Hirsch's use of the two crossed staffs with the "H". A new mark of a stylized "H" with wings and Dresden were then used by Hirsch.

Hirsch used blanks by Meissen, Rosenthal, and MZ Austria and used the gold overglaze flower to hide the manufacturer's mark.

CONFUSION ABOUT DRESDEN PORCELAIN

Many American and English collectors and dealers confuse Meissen porcelain with Dresden porcelain. Johann Frederick Böttger invented porcelain in Augustus the Strong's castle in Dresden, but the Royal Saxon Factory moved to Meissen, Germany, in about 1710. Meissen is only 14 miles from Dresden.

The confusion began in England in the early eighteenth century. Meissen porcelain was greatly in demand there and was purchased as soon as it appeared on the market. Meissen porcelain was mainly sold in the city of Dresden, as the company didn't operate a store in Meissen itself. Dresden was well known in Europe as the residence of the culture loving elector, August the Strong. Visitors to Germany stayed in Dresden, especially porcelain dealers and collectors from abroad. Since most business transactions were conducted in Dresden, the name of this city accompanied the porcelain shipped to England.

Von Schierholz

C. G. Schierholz & Sons was founded in Plaue, Thuringia in 1817. They used the four line "tit-tat-toe" mark from 1860 onward. After the family was knighted, the name was changed in 1900 to von Schierholz Porcelain Manufactory.

From about 1875 the company produced a vast number of very decorative pieces in the Meissen style. They specialized in pairs of candelabra and basket centerpieces with applied figures and flowers, similar to the work done by Carl Thieme. They copied Meissen's Purple Indian designs, rose painting and made reticulated dessert sets.

The later printed marks were variations of a crowned shield containing three oak leaves. After World War II the company came under government trusteeship and in 1972 was nationalized.

Volkstedt

This company has a complicated history, and there are at least six factories that carried the name. During the nineteenth century, table wares, decorative porcelain, coffee and tea sets and figures were produced, many in the Meissen style. In 1915 until the present, the company has specialized in decorative porcelain and figures only.

Sitzendorf

The Voight family established this porcelain manufactory in 1840 in Sitzendorf, Germany. Sitzendorf porcelain was marked with two parallel lines crossed by a third line.

The company reproduced popular Meissen models. The large decorative pieces were slip-cast rather than press-molded and are relatively light in weight compared to the heavy Meissen pieces. The general color range is more subdued with soft pastels. Cupids proliferate in Sitzendorf's decorative wares. They produced monkey band sets and pastoral figures.

Encrusted flowers played a large part in Sitzendorf's production, especially roses in delicate pinks and yellows. These contributed to the factory's success, for their output between 1870 and 1910 was vast.

Typical table centerpieces with basket tops are highly decorated with reticulation and have popular appeal. Later Sitzendorf productions are more colorful, and the factory continues to the present. Twentieth century Sitzendorf is marked with the original crossed lines, superimposed on a crowned letter S.

Sitzendorf made some lovely Meissen style figures, including elaborate figure groups. The company was semi-nationalized in 1957 and completely nationalized in 1972. The current name is VEB Sitzendorf Porcelain Manufactory.

Pair busts. Dresden, Carl Thieme, c. 1920s. Bisque busts, 4"; hand decorated in pastel shades with nice detail in Meissen style. $175.00 – 200.00

Tray, Dresden, Carl Thieme, c. 1888 – 1901. Deep, 15¼" x 12¼", magnificent hand-painted battle scene painted in eighteenth century Meissen style. $1,000.00 – 1,500.00.

Close-up of battle scene.

Demitasse cup and saucer, Dresden, Carl Thieme, c. 1901 – present. Six-footed, slightly fluted cup with twig handle, applied forget-me-nots. $250.00 – 300.00.

Cupid figure. Dresden, Carl Thieme, c. 1901 – 1960. Holding bunch of fern-like flowers, 5", applied flowers. $225.00 – 250.00.

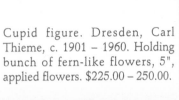

Plate, Dresden, Carl Thieme, c. 1901 – present. Reticulated, 9", center hand-painted fruit and flowers, lovely applied fruit around border. $375.00 – 400.00.

Vase, Dresden, Carl Thieme, c. 1888 – 1900. Bottle-shaped vase, possibly missing lid, hand-painted courting scenes, applied flowers. $175.00 – 200.00.

Figures of girl and boy. Dresden, Carl Thieme, c. 1920 – 1930s. 5½" to 6", girl with lamb at feet, boy with dog, hand-painted costumes. $350.00 – 400.00.

Boy.

Girl.

Demitasse pot with two cups and saucers, Dresden, Franziska Hirsch, 1901 – 1930, possible Meissen blank. Pot in Meissen style with dragon head spout, hand-painted pink roses and gilt. $500.00 – 550.00.

Covered vase, Dresden, Carl Thieme, c. 1888 – 1901. Bottle-shaped, 14"h x 6¼"w, lid with finial of encrusted leaves, vase covered with applied blue forget-me-nots, one side has hand-painted courting scene and other has array of flowers. $700.00 – 750.00.

Demitasse cup and saucer, Donath & Co., c. 1893 – 1916. Paneled quatrefoil cup 2½"w x 1¾". Deep quatrefoil saucer, 4¾"w. Medallions of courting scenes in a cobalt ground with hand gilded scrolling. $200.00 – 250.00.

Coffee cup and saucer, Dresden, Donath & Co., c. 1890s. Cup with snake handle and paw feet, hand-painted flowers, blue fish scale border. $300.00 – 350.00.

Dessert set, Meissen blank, Dresden, Donath & Co. decoration, c. 1890s. Set includes two compotes (8"w x 8"l) and six plates (8⅔"). 1¾" reticulated border with pink and aqua cut-out flowers, array of hand-painted flowers in center with gilt. $1,300.00 – 1,500.00.

Close-up of reticulation.

Covered urns, Donath & Co., c. 1890s. 5¼"h, decorated with hand-painted flowers and fish scale borders. $400.00 – 500.00.

Demitasse cup and saucer, Richard Klemm, c. 1893 – 1916. Quatrefoil cup, 2" x 2". Saucer, 4¾" x 4". Rich cobalt blue ground with gilt, courting scenes. $225.00 – 275.00.

Teacup and saucer, Ambrosius Lamm, c. 1887 – 1891. Royal Flute cup with twisted, divided, feathered handle, saucer bowl, hand-gilding on cobalt, wonderful hand-painted portrait medallion. $350.00 – 400.00.

Miniature cup and saucer, Meissen blank, probably decorated by Helena Wolfsohn, c. 1850 – 1881. Rounded cup with loop handle, cupid in reserve in purple camaieu style on yellow ground. $300.00 – 350.00.

Set of 10 plates, Meissen blank, decorated by Helena Wolfsohn, Dresden, c. 1840 – 1850. 9¾", osier border, hand-painted flowers, gilt trim. $900.00 – 1,000.00.

Single plate.

Close-up of flowers.

Trembleuse chocolate cup and saucer, Dresden, unidentified mark, c. 1870 – 1890. Scalloped cup with two ornate handles, 2⅞"w x 3". Saucer with reticulated rail, 5¼". Lid with rose bud finial with leaf extensions. Ornately hand-painted with flowers and cartouches with sailing scenes, Kutani colors. $350.00 – 375.00.

Six members of Monkey Band. Sitzendorf, c. 1930s. Each figure 4" to 5½", colorful hand-painted costumes. $100.00 – 125.00 each.

Nut set, impressed Meissen mark and "Germany." Reticulated square bowl, 8¼" with ten round individual reticulated bowls, 3¼". Hand-painted flowers and gilt trim. $350.00 – 450.00.

Close-up of one monkey.

Demitasse set, Von Schierholz, Plaue, c. 1920 – 1930s. Set includes pot, creamer, sugar, and six cups and saucers in Meissen's Royal Flute shape, decorated in Meissen's Red Indian pattern with gilt trim. $500.00 – 550.00.

Figure, Von Schierholz, c. 1907 – 1920. Lady starting to courtesy, 9¼", lace trim, hand-painted flowers on skirt. $300.00 – 350.00.

Man and woman figures, Sitzendorf, c. 1950s. 9½" each, hand decorated and enhanced by applied flowers. $500.00 – 600.00 each.

Figure of man.

Figure of woman.

Miniature cup and saucer, Hutschenreuther, c. 1920s. Cup in Royal Flute shape, transfer Blue Onion pattern. $100.00 – 125.00.

Snuff box, Volkstedt, crossed swords type mark, c. 1880s. Hinged ribbed box, 1⅞" x 1⅓", hand-painted courting scene and gilt. $100.00 – 150.00.

Covered urn, Sitzendorf, c. 1910 – 1920. Large 2-part urn with lid, 16", applied cupid on lid, two sitting cupids, transfer of courting scene on front and flowers on back. $800.00 – 900.00.

Back view of urn.

Tete-a-tete set, Von Schierholz, c. 1920s. Set includes pot in Meissen style, sugar, creamer, two cups and saucers, and a large tray, hand-painted roses and gilt. $500.00 – 600.00.

Charger, Teichert, Ernst, Meissen, 1884 – 1912. 11", artist signed, "K. Tschapek," hand-painted gypsy with flowing black hair. $500.00 – 600.00.

Handmalerei

Meissen.

Close-up of face.

Photograph of mark.

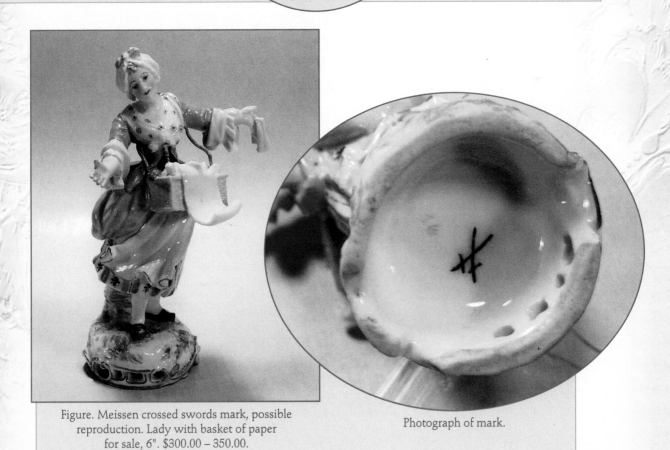

Figure. Meissen crossed swords mark, possible reproduction. Lady with basket of paper for sale, 6". $300.00 – 350.00.

Photograph of mark.

We were fortunate to visit the Meissen porcelain office in New York. We met with the president, Peter H. Jungkunst, who graciously answered many of our questions, gave us research material, and allowed us the opportunity to photograph many lovely pieces in his showroom, which we have included in this chapter.

Meissen has approximately 1,100 employees today and almost half are painters and gilders. "The company has the capability of making 150,000 different items," explained Peter. All pieces manufactured by Meissen are special ordered by customers. Examples of Meissen's line can be seen in the 12 Meissen stores throughout Europe.

We asked Peter if there was a Meissen store in the United States. "No, the United States is a difficult market for new Meissen," he replied. "The secondary market for antique Meissen is brisk in the United States, but many Americans find prices for new Meissen to be quite high. We've just reduced the prices for our dinnerware lines 30%," he explained. He believes this should help sales in the United States.

Popular dinnerware patterns such as Blue Onion, Ming Dragon, Strewn Flowers, Swan Service, Purple Indian, and Court Dragon have been reissued through the years. Ming Dragon, for example, has been produced for 100 years. "Today customers enjoying mixing and matching with different colors," states Peter. Favorite figures such as the Monkey Band are still been produced.

Meissen crossed swords dealer sign, New York showroom.

About 1,200 molds are redone each year because they wear out with continued use.

Meissen produces about 2,000 new items a year, and employs 40 product development people. They study current trends in the marketplace to come up with modern designs that fit into today's lifestyles. An example of a completely new dinnerware shape designed for the new millennium is Waves, designed by Sabine Wachs. The development of this extensive Meissen dinnerware pattern took three years. Another modern design is Orchid on a Branch, designed by Heinz Werner in 1977 and 1978.

Display case in Meissen New York showroom.

Peter showed us two new items, a large café-au-lait cup and saucer and a muesli bowl, which is used for the popular Swiss cereal or soup. There are imaginative coffee mugs for the office, lobster services, and sushi bowls to suit the way we live today.

We asked Peter about Meissen's grading system. "Kilns are computer controlled today," he explained. "There are no seconds any more, except for real small defects. These have one scratch and are sold for 20% less at the factory shop."

We wish to thank Peter H. Jungkunst, president of the New York office, for visiting with us and giving us the opportunity to take photographs. Peter retired at the end of 2003 and is enjoying his retirement in New England. A special thank you to the new president, Sabine Collins, and her assistant, Beverly Pfahlert, for their ongoing help with our endeavor.

Table top display showing Ming Dragon pattern, New York showroom.

Demitasse cup and saucer, current mark.
Cup with ring handle with thumb rest,
Wave Relief, white on white.
$45.00.

Covered sugar and creamer, current mark.
Wave Relief, white on white.
$125.00.

Coffee cup, saucer, and dessert plate, current mark.
Cup with ring handle. Saucer and dessert plate
in Waves Service, Holly pattern.
$470.00.

Candlestick. Current mark.
Waves Service, 8½",
Holly pattern.
$185.00.

Dinner plate, current mark. 10", Rich Onion
pattern, gold border. $400.00.

Bell, current mark. Waves Service, Holly
pattern. $110.00.

Figure of swan. Current mark.
4½", $600.00.

Another view.

Tureen with lid, 1¼ qt., lid with applied cupids,
swan, and flowers. Swan Service, white relief
without decoration, gold border.
$4,600.00.

Close-up of figures.

Clown, current mark. Riding unicycle, #900300, 9½"h, carrying tray with glasses, dog pulling at cape. $1,500.00.

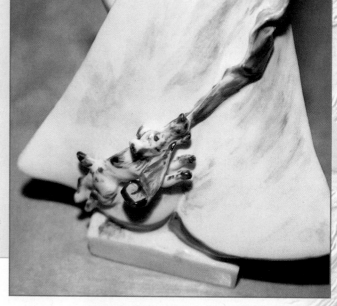

Back view of above clown, showing dog.

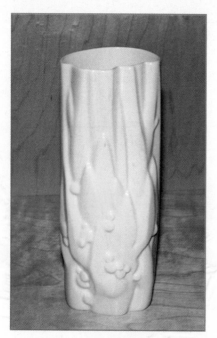

Vase, current mark. 11½", stylized flowers, White Vase collection. $150.00.

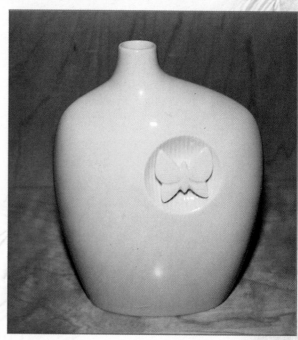

Vase, current mark, jug-shaped, 8½", medallions with carved out butterfly. $100.00.

Figure from Italian Comedy, current mark. Figure of Dottore, 7¼". $1,900.00.

Coffee cup and saucer, current mark. Cup with swan handle, 3½"h, Swan Service without decoration, gold edge and border. $220.00.

Clown music band, current mark. Ten musicians, 3½" to 4". $200.00 – 250.00 each.

Chess set, current mark. Sea World collection, pieces are various sea animals. $25,500.00.

Coffee set, current mark. Set in x-form, including coffeepot, covered sugar, creamer, one cup and one saucer, undecorated with rich gold bronze ornamentation. $1,800.00.

Dinner plate, current mark. Plate, 11", Ming Dragon, purple with gold border. $325.00 – 350.00.

Lobster platter, current mark. Scalloped, 11", hand-painted lobster. $1,200.00.

Pug dog figurine, current mark. Seated nursing baby, 6¼", blue color with bells. $1,275.00.

Pug dog, current mark. Standing, 2¾"h. $430.00.

Close-up, showing puppy.

Figurine, current mark. Bride and groom, 4". $370.00.

Teapot, current mark. Lid with rose finial, holds eight cups, Ming Dragon in yellow. $625.00.

Muesli/soup bowl, current mark. Bowl and underplate, 8¾" oz., Ming Dragon in green, gilt trim, $350.00 – 400.00.

Cockatoo figurine, current mark. 9¾". $1,600.00 – 1,650.00.

Eight square dishes, current mark. Ming Dragon in green and red, gold trim. $600.00 – 625.00 for four.

Gardening boy, current mark. Boy with grapes in back-basket, 5¼". $1,200.00 – 1,225.00.

Demitasse cup and saucer, current mark. Cup with curved handle, Arabian Nights pattern with figures, gold border. $1,300.00 – 1,325.00.

Useful Information

There are many reasons why people start a Meissen collection. Some like the thought of acquiring something that may increase in value. Others enjoy acquiring things of beauty to decorate their homes. Finally, there are those that start a collection when they receive a gift or are left something from a relative or friend. Everyone that has a collection has his or her reasons for collecting. This information is to give you some of the fine points in the art of collecting.

Knowledge

Knowledge is the key that will open many doors for you. Books, magazines, trade papers, and auction catalogs are useful tools. Many excellent books can be found in our bibliography. Talking to antique dealers and fellow collectors will help you make good decisions in your buying. Take advantage of their experience and knowledge of the subject.

Meissen, like most manufacturers, has good information on the history of the company's development and provides pictures of the items they produce. You can contact the company at:

Meissen Porcelain Inc.
41 Madison Avenue, 13th Floor
New York, NY 10010
or
Staatliche Porzellan-Manufaktur Meissen GmbH
Talstrasse 9
D-01662 Meissen
Germany

Another helpful source of information on Meissen is your computer. Do a search for "Meissen," and you will be amazed at what you will find. Meissen has a website: www.meissen.com.

If you have an interest in collecting Meissen porcelain and you are willing to do a small amount of research on the subject, you should be able to make some good buys and keep adding to your collection. Knowledge will help you know the difference between an authentic Meissen piece and a reproduction. Knowledge will also help you tell the difference between an old piece of Meissen and pieces currently being made and the value of each.

Availability

Meissen can be found at antique shows and in shops, where you will have the opportunity to talk to dealers and ask questions about items.

Auctions are good sources to find pieces to add to your collection. Preview the item carefully for flaws and damages. Remember, it is the buyer's responsibility to check the condition of an item. You must also consider the buyer's premium in figuring a bid price you are willing to pay. Above all, don't get caught up in auction fever. Plan what you want to pay, and stop there.

Internet Buying

An exciting new source for finding and buying antiques is the Internet. There are many advantages to using this method. You can shop the whole world from the comfort of your home with all your reference material handy. You have access to a worldwide market, and may find some rare and unusual pieces.

The Internet also has some disadvantages. Not being able to have a hands on inspection is certainly one of the biggest problems. Buying on the Internet alters your ability to do this. Buying from a photograph and a brief description has significantly changed the way we buy and sell antiques.

You can ask questions, but the seller may not be able to answer them properly. The seller sometimes does not have a good knowledge of what is being sold and finds it hard to describe exactly what the item is. You may have to read between the lines and ask detailed questions. Many sellers are not trained to recognize hairlines, chips, or missing gilt, and do not understand what an incised mark is or how to date a piece properly.

You must be very careful to read the fine print and understand all the conditions described. There are times that an item is sold "as is" and cannot be returned. When buying on the Internet, you should know what the return policy is. If bidding on an auction, always ask all your questions before bidding.

Inspect an item you purchased from the Internet as soon as you receive it. Some sellers only have a three-day return policy. Many items, especially Meissen figures, have been restored. A black light is a valuable tool to help you discover if an item has been restored. Run your fingers over the piece and feel for chips or cracks.

Receiving items with hairline cracks and chips is a major problem. Some sellers don't see hairlines as they can be easy to miss; this is why you should tap every piece of porcelain you buy to see if it rings. You also need a good jeweler's loupe. Always inspect a piece you get through the mail in a well lighted area.

If something is not just right, inform the seller right away and say you want to return it. A reputable dealer will refund your purchase price without any questions asked.

Condition

With any fine piece of Meissen porcelain, condition is very important. Almost all Meissen pieces have been handled and used, and therefore, can be prone to small chips, hairline cracks, and wear to the paint or gilt. Some may even have some repairs or restorations.

Hairline cracks are sometimes hard to detect. A good test is to hold the piece in one hand and tap it with your finger of your other hand; it should ring like a bell. If it thuds, there is something wrong, and you should examine the piece very carefully.

It is almost impossible to remove a fine hairline crack, although a small chip may be repairable. Handles, spouts, and finials are areas to study very carefully for repairs or regluing. Repairs to a Meissen piece are very expensive, and qualified restorers are hard to find.

Most collectors expect a small amount of gilt ware. If it is excessive, however, it could take away from its appearance, its value, or both. Minor chips on applied flowers are acceptable to most collectors. It is almost impossible to find an applied rose on a finial of a nineteenth century coffeepot or teapot that is perfect.

It is not uncommon to find examples of Meissen that have had some restorations to the fingers, hands, toes, or feet, or even replacement arms and legs. It is the quality of the piece and the quality of the restoration that is really important. Accumulating restored pieces may not hurt your collection, and you might be able to buy a rare piece at a reasonable price. A poor restoration can normally be detected.

Look for a difference in color or thickness, or an unevenness in the porcelain. If the piece is for your own collection and it looks acceptable to you, that's all that matters.

As a rule of thumb, washing a piece of Meissen should be done by hand, rather than in a dishwasher. The detergent used in dishwashers is very harsh, and the high heat in the drying cycle can cause damage to the gilt. Never use a dishwasher to wash a fine hand-painted cabinet piece of Meissen. If a piece is to be cleaned, and it does not have any restorations, you may soak it in some luke-warm water and use a mild detergent, rinse, and let dry naturally or gently pat dry with a soft towel.

A piece of Meissen is much safer if it is displayed in a closed case or cabinet. It is less likely to be touched or moved, and it will not collect dust or grease as much as an exposed piece. Pieces in cabinets will eventually need cleaning, however.

When buying a piece of Meissen, an important factor to consider is the quality of the piece. Are the colors vivid and pleasing to the eye? If the piece is a figure, are the fingers and hands well formed and is the face pleasing to you? If a piece is signed by the artist, it will usually be more valuable, although not all artists are considered equal.

If you buy a Meissen beverage set, make sure all the pieces match and the pattern numbers all agree. Make sure the colors are identical. Unfortunately, some dealers put together a marriage where pieces do not match, and they do not let the buyer know. Experience and a good eye are the best teachers.

Record Keeping

Keeping good records is very important. You should know what price you paid for each piece of Meissen as you add it to your collection. Should you decide to sell your collection, this will be useful. After each purchase, write a little note as to where it was bought and when, who sold it to you, and for how much. As your collection increases, you will have all the information on hand. You can also include historical facts about the item, such as the artist's name, period of time when it was produced, age, style, and condition. This information can easily be input on a personal computer.

Another good policy for record keeping is to photograph your Meissen collection. This will be useful for insurance purposes. It's also easier to show your pieces off to fellow collectors through photographs instead of carrying the piece around. It helps to have a photograph on hand if you want to trade for pieces you don't have.

Protection

As your Meissen collection increases and hopefully becomes more valuable, you should consider purchasing insurance. Just think what your loss would be if there were a fire or theft. Nothing would be covered if you didn't have fine arts coverage added to your homeowner's insurance policy. If your insurance company requires an outside appraiser, you should hire a qualified person with recognized credentials. Look for one in your local telephone directory. Look under "appraisers" or "antique dealers." You may also be able to get a recommendation from an antique dealer or your insurance company.

Display

Your Meissen collection will enhance the décor of your home when properly displayed. As Meissen porcelain figures are fragile, they are best displayed in a glass-enclosed curio cabinet. Shadow boxes and wall sconces also make attractive ways to showcase your special pieces of Meissen. Never store fine porcelain in a very hot or very cold location, as any sudden changes in temperature could possible crack the glaze.

You may want to buy plate stands or hangers to display your Meissen set. They are available in a wide assortment of styles and configurations to suite your taste. They can be purchased at antique shows, on the Internet, or at local gift shops or hardware stores.

Remember to keep your precious collection out of reach of small children and pets. If you use a cleaning service, point out your fragile pieces to them. It is probably best to clean them yourself.

Bibliography

Adams, Len & Yvonne. *Meissen Portrait Figures*. London, England: Barrie & Jenkins, 1987.

Bagdade, Susan and Al. *Warman's English and Continental Pottery and Porcelain*. Iola, WI: Krause Publications, 1998.

Ballay, Ute. "Paul Scheurich at Meissen." *Antiques & Collecting*, 4/98.

Begg, Patricia, John Scarce, and Harry Blackburn. *Flowers of Fantasy: Three Centuries of Flower Painting*. Ceramics and Glass Circle of Australia, 1997.

Berling, Dr. K. *Meissen China: An Illustrated History*. New York, NY: Dover Publications, Inc., 1972.

Den Blaawuen, Abraham L. *Meissen Porcelain in the Rijksmuseum*. Amsterdam: Waanders Publishers, 2000.

Fay-Halle, Antoinette and Barbara Mundt. *Porcelain of the Nineteenth Century*. New York, NY: Rizzoli, 1983.

Geissler, Uwe. *Painting Porcelain in the Meissen Style*. Atglen, PA: Schiffer Publishing Ltd., 1997.

Godden, Geoffrey. *Godden's Guide to European Porcelain*. New York, NY: Cross River Press, 1993.

Hallwag. *Meissen Porcelain*. Berne, Switzerland: 1969.

Harran, Jim and Susan. *Dresden Porcelain Studios*. Paducah, KY: Collector Books, 2002.

_____. *Collectible Cups & Saucers Books I, II, and III*. Paducah, KY: Collector Books, 1998 – 2003.

Hesni, Deloris. *The H. Lloyd Hawkins, Jr. Meissen Collection*. New Orleans, LA: New Orleans Museum of Art, 1997.

Honey, William B. *Dresden China*. Troy, New York: David Rosenfeld, 1946.

Hutton, William. "Kaendler at Meissen." *Discovering Antiques*. New York: Greystone Press, 1973.

Jones, Simon. "Flights of Fancy Count Brühl and the Swan Service." *Antiques & Collecting*, 12/2000

Menzhausen, Ingelore. *Early Meissen Porcelain in Dresden*. Berlin, Germany: Henschelverlag Kunst und Gesellschaft, 1990.

Michael, George. "The Magic of Meissen." *Antiques & Collecting*, 11/99.

Michenhagen, Dr. R. *German Porcelain*. Munich, Germany: Gogath & Sohn.

Mitchell, Laurence. "A Service for the Collector." Internet site no longer available.

Morley-Fletcher, Hugo. *Antique Porcelain in Color*. Garden City, NY: Doubleday & Co., Inc., 1971.

Raffo, Pietro. "Meissen in Transition and Decline." *Discovering Antiques*. New York: Greystone Press, 1973.

Rogers, William. "The Porcelain Figures of Meissen." *Antique Trader Annual of Articles of Antiques, Vol. VII*, 1977.

Röntgen, Robert E. *The Book of Meissen*. Atglen, PA: Schiffler Publishing Ltd., 1984.

Schärer, Jurgen. *Meissen 75*. VEB Staatliche. Porzellan-Manufaktur Meissen, Meissen, Germany, 1975.

Sonntag, Dr. Hans and Betty Schuster. *MeiBen and Meissen, Europe's Oldest Porcelain Manufactory*. Gutersloh, Germany: Mohndruck Graphische Betriebe, 1991.

Verlag, R. V. *Meiben & Meissen*. Berlin, Germany: Mohndruck Graphische Betriebe, 1991.

Walcha, Otto. *Meissen Porcelain*. New York, NY: G. P. Putnam's Sons, 1981.

Ware, George W. *German and Austrian Porcelain*. New York, NY: Crown Publishers, 1963.

Wark, Ralph and Mary Campbell Grisina. *The War Collection: Early Meissen Porcelain*. Jacksonville, FL: The Cummer Gallery of Art, 1984.

_____. "BBC Painting Flowers: The Rose." Internet: www.bbc.co.uk/bbcfour/paintingflowers/flower_type/rose.html.

_____. "The Dragon and the Quail: English Kakeimon Porcelain." Stockspring Antiques, London. Internet: http://www.porcelainexhibition.com/Introduction.htm.

_____. "Meissen Porcelain." Internet: www.meissen.com.

_____. "Meissen Indian Decorations. Internet: www.vingerhaeden.nl/start/ander/eng1.htm.

_____. "Meissen Porcelain from a European Private Collection." Sotheby's Catalog, 1997.

_____. "Meissen Porcelain 1710 – 1754." The Ceramic Bulletin of the China Students' Club of Boston, 9/66.

_____. "Meissen Porcelain, White Gold with Blue Swords." VEB Staatliche. Porzellan-Manufaktur Meissen GDR, 1970s.

_____. "Nineteenth Century Meissen." *Antiques & Collecting*, 6/97.

_____. "A Passion for Porcelain: Three Centuries of Meissen Floral Painting." Haggerty Museum of Art Past Exhibitions. Internet:www.marquethe.edu/haggerty/exhibitions/past/meissen/meissen.html.

_____. Pattern Books, The Tableware Collections, *Mahonia Garland Pattern, Vinium Orchid on a Branch, B Form X Form, Ornate Indian Painting, Ming Dragon Playing with Pearl, Vine Leaf Garland, Paris Peddlers, Gallant Orchestra, Monkey Orchestra, Gardener Children, Colorful Birds,* Staatliche. Porzellan-Manufaktur Meissen, Meissen, Germany.

_____. "Porcelain Manufacturing," and "Over Glaze Decorating – The Gold Painter. Internet: www.meissen.de/eng/html.

_____. "Rose Stories, Rose Tales, Rose Legends..." Internet: www.rose.co.uk.html. 12/29/02.

_____. *Staatliche Porzellan-Manufaktur Meissen.*

Index

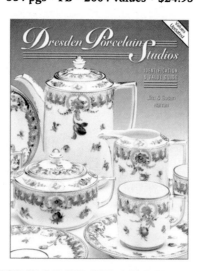

COLLECTOR BOOKS
informing today's collector

www.collectorbooks.com

For over two decades we have been keeping collectors informed on trends and values in all fields of antiques and collectibles.

BOOKS ON POTTERY, PORCELAIN & FIGURINES

4844 American **Painted Porcelain**, Kamm $19.95
4929 **American Art Pottery**, 1880 – 1950, Sigafoose $24.95
6549 **California Pottery Scrapbook**, Chipman $29.95
4851 Collectible **Cups & Saucers**, Harran $18.95
5529 Collectible **Cups & Saucers**, Book II, Harran $19.95
6326 Collectible **Cups & Saucers**, Book III, Harran $24.95
6344 Collectible **Vernon Kilns**, 2nd Edition, Nelson......................$29.95
6331 Collecting **Head Vases**, Barron............................$24.95
6621 Coll. Ency. of **American Dinnerware**, 2nd Ed., Cunningham ..$29.95
4931 **Collector's Encyclopedia of Bauer Pottery**, Chipman $24.95
5034 Collector's Ency. of **California Pottery**, 2nd Ed.,Chipman $24.95
5917 **Collector's Encyclopedia of Russel Wright**, Kerr $29.95
5910 Collector's Encyclopedia of **English China**, Gaston............$29.95
6629 Collector's Encyclopedia of **Fiesta**, 10th Ed., Huxford $24.95
6637 Collector's Ency. of **Made in Japan Ceramics**, White........$24.95
5824 Collector's Encyclopedia of **Hall China**, 3rd Ed., Whitmyer....$29.95
3431 Collector's Ency. of **Homer Laughlin China**, Jasper..........$24.95
1276 Collector's Encyclopedia of **Hull Pottery**, Roberts..............$19.95
5609 Collector's Ency. of **Limoges Porcelain**, 3rd Ed., Gaston $29.95
2334 Collector's Encyclopedia of **Majolica Pottery**, Katz-Marks ...$19.95
5831 Collector's Encyclopedia of **Metlox Potteries**, 2nd Ed., Gibbs.$29.95
5270 Collector's Encyclopedia of **Muncie Pottery**, Rans/Eckelman..$24.95
5677 Collector's Encyclopedia of **Niloak**, 2nd Edition, Gifford.........$29.95
5679 Collector's Encyclopedia of **Red Wing Art Pottery**, Dollen .$24.95
5618 Collector's Encyclopedia of **Rosemeade Pottery**, Dommel.$24.95
5841 Collector's Ency. of **Roseville Pottery**, Huxford/Nickel $24.95
5842 Coll. Ency. of **Roseville Pottery**, Vol. 2., Huxford/Nickel $24.95
6646 Collector's Encyclopedia of **Stangl Artware, Lamps & Birds**,
      2nd Edition, Runge $29.95
3314 Collector's Ency. of **Van Briggle Art Pottery**, Sasicki $24.95
5255 Collector's Guide to **Camark Pottery**, Book II, Gifford $19.95
5680 Collector's Guide to **Feather Edge Ware**, McAllister $19.95
4860 Collector's Gde. to **Homer Laughlin's Virginia Rose**, Racheter.. $18.95

6124 Coll. Guide to **Made In Japan Ceramics**, Book IV, White ...$24.95
4954 Collector's Guide to **Souvenir China**, Williams $19.95
6244 Collector's Guide to **Yellow Ware**, McAllister/Michel $19.95
4734 Collector's Guide to **Yellow Ware**, Book II, McAllister $17.95
6245 Collector's Guide to **Yellow Ware**, Book III, McAllister $19.95
6634 Collector's Ultimate Ency. of **Hull Pottery**, Roberts............$29.95
1425 **Cookie Jars**, Westfall $9.95
6316 Decorative **American Pottery & Whiteware**, Wilby $29.95
5909 **Dresden Porcelain** Studios, Harran $29.95
6320 Gaston's **Blue Willow**, 3rd Edition $19.95
6630 Gaston's **Flow Blue China**, Gaston $29.95
1917 **Head Vases**, Cole $14.95
2379 Lehner's Ency. of **U.S. Marks** on Pottery, Porcelain & China ..$24.95
4722 **McCoy Pottery**, Coll. Reference & Value Guide, Hanson ...$19.95
5268 **McCoy Pottery**, Volume II, Hanson/Nissen $24.95
5913 **McCoy Pottery**, Volume II, Hanson/Nissen $24.95
6333 **McCoy Pottery Wall Pockets** & Decorations, Nissen $24.95
6835 **Meissen Porcelain**, Harran...$29.95
6135 **North Carolina** Art Pottery, 1900 – 1960, James/Leftwich $24.95
5834 **Occupied Japan** Collectibles, Florence $24.95
6335 Pictorial Guide to **Pottery & Porcelain**, Marks, Lage $29.95
5691 **Post86 Fiesta**, Identification & Value Guide, Racheter $19.95
1670 **Red Wing** Collectibles, DePasquale $9.95
1440 **Red Wing Stoneware**, DePasquale $9.95
6037 **Rookwood Pottery**, Nicholson/Thomas........................$24.95
6287 **Roseville Pottery** Price Guide, No. 13, Huxford $12.95
6838 **R. S. Prussia & More**, McCaslin $29.95
3738 **Shawnee Pottery**, Mangus $24.95
6828 The Ultimate Collector's Ency. of **Cookie Jars**, Roerig..........$29.95
6640 Van Patten's **ABC's of Collecting Nippon Porcelain**,...$29.95
3327 **Watt Pottery**, Identification & Value Guide, Morris $19.95
5924 **Zanesville Stoneware** Company, Rans/Ralston/Russell $24.95

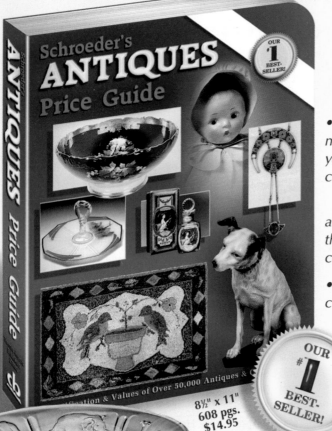